From

Math Anxiety

to

Mastery

in 6 stages

STAGE 2

Encoding Conceptual Understanding

SHAD MOARIF

Please go to our Companion website www.karismath.com for links to purchase the following set of Books on Amazon:

STAGE 1: Encoding Mathematical Symbolisms
STAGE 2: Encoding Conceptual Understanding
STAGE 3: Processing Numbers
STAGE 4: Mathematical Operations
STAGE 5: Algorithmic Thinking
STAGE 6: Problem-Solving

Karismath videos can be viewed at the site that explain Math concepts, procedures and operations while demonstrating how to teach them. All Karismath videos, from Grade 1 to Grade 5 are on every math topic and available as free streaming videos.

All graphic-visuals content in the books to demonstrate mathematical concepts have been produced by Shad Moarif, Founder-Developer, Karismath.

Cover and book design by Alexandru Oprescu

ISBN: 978-1-3999-4299-7

First published 2022

TABLE OF CONTENTS

Dedicated to the memory of
Khaleda Moarif
Paulette Moarif

and to my dearest wife
Anjana Raza

and children
Ayesha and Sara

The population today divides sharply into those who hate and fear mathematics and a minority of mathematicians.

The remarkable thing is that such an outcome is accepted as normal. It is as if physical education cripples 90% of the children taking it.

W.W. Sawyer, (1958)
'The Possibility of Universal Mathematical Literacy'

Preface

In 1997 I conducted a private experiment quite unintentionally, caused by a turn of fate in my personal circumstances. While languishing in the isolation of the workless, I had an attack of curiosity: "*What if I were to write down all that I do in my training workshops and seminars when explaining what Fractions meant, the different types of fractions, their four operations, etc? What if I wrote down the pedagogy that was prescribed by the topic itself, with all its nuances? How many pages would it take in print form?*"

Three months and 762 foolscap pages later, my printer rolled out 381 double-sided pages for me to ponder, as my "*Book of Fractions.*"

The biggest take from this experiment:

1. When teaching math, every math topic like Fractions, generates its topic-oriented pedagogy. Pedagogy is the mantle that teachers wrap around every contour of the topic to make its invisible inner structure appear clearly visible and audible.
2. The mantle of pedagogy that enrobes a math topic carries numerical and symbolic patterns. These contain distinctive terms, definitive symbols and operations unique to the topic. Teachers use it with their students to unravel the hidden intricacies of mathematical content captured inside the mantle.
3. Content and pedagogy together constitute the *mathematical knowledge* contained in a topic.

Fast-forward nine years later to Singapore which is 2nd (after China) in PISA's rankings for math performance by countries. Since 2006 Singapore has been publishing high-quality Primary and Middle Math textbooks (intended for elite schools). Their math textbooks devoted a total of almost 200 pages to Fractions. Approximately 60% of the content carried instructional visualization in color. All their math textbooks came with Practice Worksheets that made up 68% of their math content. This helped them achieve 80-90% of their high curriculum standards for all their state schools.

By contrast, and 15 years later (2011), high quality Math textbooks designed for top elite schools in Pakistan, were devoting less than 60 pages to Fractions with less than 1% devoted to instructional visualization.

Even when given a wide berth, developing countries like Pakistan are offering approximately 30% of mathematical knowledge needed for mastery of a foundational topic in their elite schools. Teachers are expected to fill in the missing 70%. If one takes into account Government state schools, the mathematical knowledge contained in their math textbooks crashes to almost 5%. Government school teachers (often semi-educated) are expected to plug a deficit of 95%. Very few well-educated math teachers successfully manage the 70% deficit in elitist schools. As in much of South-East Asia, the deficits are addressed via expensive private tuition after school.

This legacy of the missing 70% has been passed down to schools everywhere in the world since the 19th century when research in math teaching and learning was almost non-existent. The mathematics curriculum expected schools to provide mathematical knowledge that would prepare the future citizenry to study the hard sciences. The best math Textbooks, were approved and selected for the purpose. Student assessments and examinations were administered to test if schools were delivering according to the requirements of the curriculum.

However, when we join the dots, we end up associating mathematical knowledge with math textbooks that contained 30% of it in the best cases. In terms of a jigsaw puzzle of a 1000 pieces, more than 50% of the Big-Picture pieces, along with their granular details, were missing. Student assessments and exams were doomed to test students' ignorance, not knowledge of mathematics.

This is because for much of the 20th century, trainers and practitioners inherited the same legacy of having to explain the unwritten, and the unknown, in primary and middle level math textbooks. A lot of effort was spent on understanding the logic of mathematical operations that were disembodied from conceptual understanding. Understandably, therefore, the concerns of experienced practitioners-turned-trainers converged upon:

a) How can learners be helped to remember the rules that govern math operations?
b) How can one emphasise the presence of abstract logical thinking in more user-friendly ways?

No one came even close to answering the question that almost all students were thinking about but never asking: "*Why are we doing all this*?" The answers were unconvincing specially when trainers fell down the slippery slope of jaded cliches to explain why, taking the teachers and students with them. And it was nobody's fault. Math text-books have to manage weight and volume of the book first. The knowledge in it is modified accordingly.

The "Deficits" Legacy

In his 1946 lecture on "The Teaching of Mathematics," W.W. Sawyer stated:

> *The teacher stands at the blackboard. It is perfectly clear to him what the symbols mean, and what conclusion can be drawn from them. It is completely otherwise with many of the pupils. What the symbols are meant to represent, how the teacher knows what is right and what is wrong, what is the object of the whole business anyway—all this is wrapped in mystery. The great majority of students say to themselves, "We shall never learn this stuff, but we want to get through the exam. We'll have to learn it by heart." (WW Sawyer, 1946)*

Teacher-trainers and trainers inherited the deficits legacy. They all grew up learning Math with the same handicaps in math textbooks as others. They could empathise with the terrible dread school students had for mathematics. As in their own days of schooling, early mathematical concepts could be best understood with hindsight many years later in high school or college. Previous generations of teachers, were a stoic lot. They respected the sparse diet of Math in textbooks and made up for it by exercising authority over their students. But all who were concerned about the growing anxiety around mathematics learning, agreed upon one mission: have their students pass their exams as prescribed by the math curriculum. Continued math failure in examinations had to be averted somehow.

By the middle of the 20th century math education pivoted frantically around the math curriculum, math tests and exams and students' performance. Student success became the mantra because it validated the curriculum's needs. Teachers were doing the right thing. If failure rates were high it was because, well, "a majority of the students in schools everywhere are dense."

During the decades that followed, a growing consensus emerged about the *real* problem with math in schools: it needed continuous improvements in presenting mathematical operations sequences more consistently and logically, from the simple to the complex. It called for reforming the curriculum to displace the rote-n-learn, chalk-n-talk pedagogy with one that pivoted towards greater conceptual understanding and problem-solving. The task of designing and creating such a pedagogy, despite huge chunks of missing mathematical knowledge, was passed on to the teachers in the spirit of offering them poetic license. While they felt entitled to it, they were also increasingly burdened by it.

Trainers and teachers were supposed to generate the rest of the mathematical jigsaw pieces by extending whatever they had, as logically as possible. They had to turn them into elastic, flexible pieces by over-emphasising their conceptual aspects. This risks inviting overkill.

Not much has changed since, in terms of schooling the world over, specially in the developing world which copy-paste western attempts at math education reforms habitually, without thinking. Those who suffer the most are a vast (and growing) majority attending state schools. Mathematics continues to be associated with the highest levels of student failure, despite enormous improvements in the look-and-feel of textbooks. Teachers in general are far more insightful today but Math teachers are struggling harder than ever before. Much to their credit, they have grown more eclectic when filling in the missing 50%-*plus* of mathematical knowledge with supplementary materials offered at training seminars, workshops and conferences. Now with Google and the internet, their steps are turning into strides.

However, the longest, most advanced strides have been taken mainly in developing guiding principles for general pedagogy. Few doubt that pedagogical practices remain instrumental in improving students' performance. It proved itself in teaching Language, Arts, History, Science, Literature... etc. Most well-educated adults, with a little bit of training, can understand almost all non-mathematical related school subjects simply by reading up on them. Teachers and parents can increase their knowledge of learning how to teach them by understanding how best children learn them.

Not so with mathematics.

The Seven Principles of Sound General Pedagogy

Here are the seven essential principles of pedagogy, probably among the finest being advocated today. Each one of them inspires teachers to pursue excellence in math learning and dispel anxiety. But each principle is compromised by the absence of critical pieces of mathematical knowledge. Such knowledge deficits seriously hamper earnest efforts at practicing enlightened pedagogical approaches.

Principle 1

Make your teaching *learner-centric*: Don't teach Math. Teach Johnny. Regard your student as your prime subject. It is not students who should adapt their learning to the needs of Math but Math that should be adapted to the needs of the students.

Comment 1

It is unrealistic to expect teachers to demonstrate the expertise needed to adapt their Math teaching to the needs of the learner. Those needs, more often than not, tap mostly into areas relating to the 50%-plus of missing math pieces.

Principle 2

Switch to *inquiry-oriented* mode: ask questions to provoke connections that can point them towards what they are seeking to understand.

Comment 2

It is difficult for teachers to frame their question in ways that provoke mathematical connections if their understanding falls short. Teacher anxiety rises due to fears of not satisfying their students' curiosity. Trainers and teachers feel more confident when they can successfully transform student curiosity into student interest and motivation. This is hard to carry out when working with aspects that deploy soulless mathematical operations. Teasing out the missing pieces solely with math operation tools can cause pedagogical overkills..

Principle 3

Use *formative assessments*: teach by checking if students are headed in the direction of the target concept (or operation). If they deviate and stumble, modify your teaching practices to blend with your students' learning styles.

Comment 3

Guru teachers who conduct formative assessments while teaching, bring a sound knowledge of math just as a piano teacher brings sound (no pun unintended) musical knowledge across four domains: knowledge of the instrument, of piano-playing, of music, and how to help students acquire mastery in it. She can be flexible and customise her approaches across these four aspects of theory and practice. Such an approach may be too much to expect from most math teachers who work under pressure, and are anxious for all the right reasons. Many spend their leisure time scouting the internet, struggling to plug knowledge-deficits they inherited like a loan they never asked for in the first place. For others, such as myself, it was like being asked to learn ... then teach ... how to pour tea expertly without spilling a drop, using teapots with spouts and handles on the same side. Flawed tools provoke risky practices.

Principle 4

Make them *think critically*: make students think *between the lines* (i.e. between the bits they understand), to help them turn implicit connections into explicit ones. Extraneous, distracting information should be filtered out via simple reasoning.

Comment 4

This is almost impossible to do if teachers find it very challenging to follow the pedagogical practices prescribed in 1, 2 and 3 above. Critical thinking requires sifting the extraneous from the necessary, the important from the unimportant, the logical from the illogical. All these choices have to be curated at very granular levels during mathematical processes. They involve executive decision-making ("*What is being asked here? What is the big picture?*"). Some of these are procedural ("*Should **x** be divided first or should **y** be reduced first?*"). Others are conceptual (*"How can one divide a small amount with a larger amount as in fractions?")* or operational ("*Should the next step be recorded as* ***abc*** *or* ***xyz****?*").

How can one think critically when serious knowledge-deficits straddle areas where even reasoning feels wobbly?

Principle 5

Work as a team: form groups to harness the collective intelligence of team members to fill in the missing links in each other's understanding. Analyze and synthesize ideas for better understanding.

Comment 5

Forming groups is not difficult. To curate individual inputs and tease out an appealing tapestry of collective intelligence that keeps the process going, demands special skills and much training. It is not difficult to learn but it does assume that teachers will come with an expert knowledge of mathematics.

Principle 6

Turn such teaching-learning experiences into constructivist problem-solving exercises. Students should be helped to own the task of connecting all the missing links and connections in their understanding of math concepts and operations. When they do, they will intuitively resort to personal heuristics to solve math problems.

Comment 6

In the present context, this can be misconstrued to mean: *"let the kids figure out the missing knowledge by being creative."* Constructivism is a powerful idea. Those who engage in it work with what they understand. Their understanding becomes the vehicle to take them to pastures where new knowledge and insights await harvesting. Constructivism invites meaning-making at every stage of de-construction, construction and re-construction. But teachers and students must begin with what they know and understand deeply and well. It is almost impossible to make meaning out of something that is not well understood to begin with. It is like expecting a 5-6 year old to phonically decode, for the first time, alphabet-sounds which, when joined together and sounded out, carry no meaning: instead of decoding /b/-/e/-/d/ he is asked to decode /p/-/u/-/n/!

Principle 7

Always consider assessing the student's learning style. One may respond to a visual approach, another to an auditory or tactile approach. Many others would use a combination of two or three approaches with one more dominant than the others.

Comment 7

Learning styles are more reliable when a learner displays a certain sensory bias in *understanding* a mathematical concept. When learners struggle to understand them and fail, concepts get murkier. A cognitive struggle, propelled by a desperate need to understand mathematics under pressure, summons all three senses: touch, sight, sound. One is trying *everything in every way* to understand, not out of choice but necessity. When students struggle to understand math this way, their efforts need not reflect any particular learning style.

When teachers and students experience minimal or no struggle in understanding, it suggests little or no cognitive resistance. In such cases, they are more likely to use their own true learning style because it is clealy working. How much, how well, how quickly and how deeply they understand may still vary in terms of how *quickly* they learn:

i) The *same* pedagogical principle when applied *orally* using just numbers and no visuals may be understood faster or slower by some.
ii) The *same* pedagogical principle when applied *visually* may be understood faster or slower by some.
iii) The *same pedagogical principle* when applied using the *tactile touch-n-feel* approach may be understood faster or slower by some.

However, differences in how *much* they learn, how *well* and how *deeply*, may not be very significant.

By the same token, very differing pedagogies, made diverse by considerable variability in the conceptualisation and understanding of math concepts, can provoke learning styles that may be transitional and therefore, less authentic. In such cases, the differences in how much they learn, how well and how deeply, may be quite significant.

What the Six Stages Offer

The book on Six Stages attempts to offer a new beginning to address the pervasive anxiety that teachers and students share among themselves about teaching and learning primary and middle school mathematics. It offers the source-code for the missing 50%-*plus* of knowledge deficits passed down from generation to generation, from trainers to teachers and parents to children. The Six Stages offer, not food for thought about reforms in mathematics education, but in large part, critical aspects of the reforms themselves. During the mid-90's, W.W.Sawyer was a lone voice in the wilderness. He went about explaining the how's and why's of mathematics education at all levels, in many countries.

His voice has been heard. Today, in the 21st century, efforts are afoot everywhere, to bring to mathematics teacher-training the missing pieces of mathematical knowledge the world inherited as a liability in the Accountability Ledger. From trainers to teachers, thinkers and writers, think-tanks and edu-tech pioneers, everyone is pitching in to make the learning of mathematics meaningful to everybody. The great paradigm shift has taken place.

Mathematics and Math teachers can be made universal, just as W.W. Sawyer envisioned. It is happening. If primary and middle mathematics can be imagined to be a ship, it has been sinking for some time, burdened by a weight of History it can no longer bear. Now that we are throwing much of it overboard, my book: "From Anxiety to Math Mastery in Six Stages" comes as part of a new crew. We are here with the others, to replace old, sputtering engines with brand new sails.

SHAD MOARIF
Ed.M, Harvard University
November 5, 2022

Introduction to THE SIX STAGES TO MASTERY

I. THE PROBLEM

Children are not born inside cradles of anxiety. But, by the time they hit Grade 3 in school, they notice how adults in authority get nervous around numbers. From siblings ("*Go ask Mom!*"), to Moms ("*Go ask Dad!*"), Dads ("*Go ask the teacher!*"), teachers ("*Maybe check the internet?*") and friends ("*Did you ask your tutor?*"), school-going children stumble into a population of adults who grapple with numbers and math as with no other subject. Many hate math, and dislike it still. Math anxiety, it would seem, mirrors the expressions of math-anxious adults all around them.

Society and culture has watermarked math anxiety in children's minds from the very start, long before they open their first math textbooks. Among its many possible causes, four can be traced to the design of textbooks and pedagogy:

(a) ***conventional representations of math topics*** fail to capture the deeper reasoning that connect mathematical ideas.

(b) ***conventional teaching*** remains shy of important insights coming out of neuro-cognition research on how growing minds learn mathematics and how they use language to process numbers in order to reason numerically.

(c) ***the pervasive presence of chronic math anxiety*** itself plunges learners into a combustible world of distress, fear, worry and self-doubt. Most engage in expending a lot of emotional labor. As a result, anxiety-management issues impede their focus on math learning.

Mathematics teaching and learning can be viewed from different perspectives. It depends on who is doing the viewing. Software developers and financial engineers would propose their own curriculum. Rocket scientists and genetic engineers may conceptualise it differently while games-developers and statisticians might offer their own perspectives.

STEM learning (Science, Technology, Engineering and Mathematics) places Math as one would place the father or the son in a family portrait. It is a portrait framed by history. But it also serves as the vision statement for learning mathematics. The interests of professionals involved with the teaching of hard sciences are naturally invested in the goals of math education, in what should be taught and why. These are visionaries whose predecessors established long ago that the future trajectory of the world will continue to curve in the direction of technological advancement.

Be as it may, the inherent architecture of mathematics does not change. Regardless of motives, goals and causes, students still need to learn place-values, the four operations, fractions, decimals and percentages, geometry, trigonometry and algebra. There is no avoiding it. Whether one aspires to conquer outer space or dream of making the earth a better place to live in, the basic building blocks remain numbers. They are as generic to math as clay is to porcelain. There is a natural order to numbers that only the cross-pollination of mathematics and the mind can capture.

It is understandable if primary and middle-school teachers choose to be agnostic about vision statements. They feel distant because the children in their classrooms stand quite far removed from their finishing-school phase and sit much closer in their starting-school phase. Primary and middle school minds are jostled by more compelling questions: "How should we teach a tough subject like mathematics to these children?" Those like us, who believe we know how, sometimes wonder: "How should future learners themselves describe mathematics one day, long after they learned mathematics from us?":

> *"When asked to describe mathematics, they should say something like 'It's about ways for solving problems', instead of 'It's about triangles' or 'solving equations' or 'doing percent.' (Cuoco and Goldenberg: "Habits of Mind," 1996)*

The above statement captures something generic and essential about how the mathematical mind works. Today there is a growing minority of theoreticians and practitioners who are able to offer glimpses into the inner architecture of mathematics. Its exploration by young minds can cultivate a "habit of mind" capable of developing "ways for solving problems": complex ones that require the ability to deconstruct the old in order to reconstruct the new, using mathematical approaches.

> *"Students should develop the habit of taking ideas apart and putting them back together. When they do this, they should want to see what happens if something is left out or if the pieces are put back in a different way." (Cuoco and Goldenberg: "Habits of Mind," 1996)*

The proximity of primary and middle school teachers to school-starting students brings them face to face with another common conundrum: What should one do to align one's teaching to student learning? This alignment can be imagined as the Socket-and-Plug model where the Socket represents the learners' readiness to receive mathematical ideas as active learners. The Plug represents mathematics courseware which is instructionally designed to fit the students' preparedness for math learning. Together they ought to disentangle complex mathematical knots to produce a seamless, resistance-free flow of mathematics learning. In attempting to do this, math trainers and teachers are bringing to attention the need to develop a unique educator's perspective on how mathematics should be taught in primary and middle school.

A coherent and cohesive pedagogy that aligns primary and secondary math teaching can lead to success when five indispensable elements are harnessed:

a) Teachers' *knowledge and mastery of math* content in all topics in terms of concepts and operations, and their applications in problem solving.

b) A knowledge of *how minds understand and process numerical quantities* using verbal, visual and numerical reasoning.

c) An understanding of the *developmental aspects* of children's cognitive and psychological growth.

d) Pedagogical approaches designed to *encode and decode numerical information* simply and meaningfully.

e) Instructional design that employs *static and dynamic imagery to articulate mathematical forms.* These should resonate deep inside the rational-intuitive Deep Knowledge System (DKS) of learners.

There remains the sticky and fiddly issue of children's "learning styles." When we try unscrambling *"How does Johnny learn numbers?"* or *"How does Ayesha learn part-whole relationships?"* Much of what we discern suggests patterns of learning that can be traced to patterns of earlier teaching by parents, teachers or other adults who themselves may display certain preferences: verbal, visual, or tactile. These leave a corresponding imprint upon Johnny's and Ayesha's learning and display unmistakable similarities.

How do mathematical concepts originate *without* received instruction? Can one imagine a new-born baby's cognitive landscape to be pristine and unblemished by previously embossed learning? How does such a perfect cognitive surface respond to external stimuli falling upon its surface for the first time in its life? Is there a source-code that prompts a newborn's ability to judge mathematical precepts like *"less and more"*?

The Six Stages offer an insightful understanding of these issues.

II. MASTERY IN MATHEMATICS

Mastery is skills-specific across different domains like sports, music, arts and science.

The talent, skills and practice needed to achieve mastery in playing snooker is different from that needed to become an accomplished guitarist. Both engage different muscles of the heart, head and limb. Viewed in this context, mastery in almost all domains assumes the existence of a tangible instrument to master. It could be a racquet, a violin, or a paintbrush. Their design, the materials they are made of, their construction, all these contribute to the efforts to achieve mastery. A violinist who has performed before international audiences in the main capitals of the world would probably be the most promising resource to groom a novice to stardom. By the same token, if a dentist had to make her own dental tools to practice her profession, a lot of unforced errors would creep into her construction of home-crafted tools. Their use would result in flawed practices. No matter how good her knowledge is, or how competent her fine motor-skills are, she is simply not equipped to construct medical instruments.

However, soccer players have only their bodies, and singers, only their voices, as their instrument. They embody the tool. When singers achieve mastery they aspire to become divas and maestros. They can spend a lifetime training their voice as their embodied musical instrument.

Mathematics teachers have neither an external instrument nor an internal tool to master. They have only mathematics. How can students in the classroom achieve mastery in mathematics? It is possible only when their teachers pass on to students what they themselves possess: mastery over mathematics, just like a diva or a maestro.

The achievement of mastery in school mathematics is possible when learners rid themselves of anxiety, that stubborn bottleneck that blocks the psychic flow of energy. It unravels a slow but sure process when mathematics learning gets deconstructed into its Six Stages. Each stage converts hidden abilities into useful skills that require a different brand of mastery. The journey from stage to stage inspires confidence and clarity in mathematical thinking. The understanding in each skill set blends with a higher skill set until all six harmonise musically with the beat and pace of an orchestra. Such a process embodies an orchestra inside the music director, who is the teacher. To achieve mastery, the teacher has to be the medium and the message, the director and the instrument, the person and the player, the heart and the mind, the singer and the song.

III. THE SIX STAGES

In my 35 years of practice, I worked in clinical settings with an extremely diverse population of learners. It includes many who were chronic under-achievers and some with mathematics learning difficulties (dyscalculic), a majority of whom were gifted. Almost all of them disliked math intensely. My students and teachers, aged between 5 and 60, came from Canada, the U.S, Pakistan, France, the UK, Bangladesh, Singapore and Kenya, many with English as their second language.

During my three decades as a private mathematics teacher and math teacher-trainer I found I was dealing with three types of impediments in math learning:

a) The first stems from *the nature of the subject itself*: mathematics contains certain features in which *numbers* and *symbols, concepts* and *operations* appear to behave in mysterious ways. These four strands of math seem to veer off in different directions like as if they had been quarrelling among themselves.

b) The second stems from *the nature and personality of distressed learners*: They internalise their difficulties by blaming themselves: *"I am stupid or lazy, quite incapable of learning math or all of the above. I deserved to be punished!"* Such self-deprecatory attitudes pickle for years in an addictive brew of fear, anxiety and anger. Anxiety becomes a chronic state of heart and head, provoked by the very word "mathematics." It has the power to mangle the thinking process.

c) The third stems from *the nature and experience of math-learning at home and school:* Parental and societal pressures feel psychologically punitive. Most under-performers find it hard to explain: "*What* don't you understand? *Why* don't you understand it?" They can't summon the courage to declare their plight because they are plagued by chronic anxiety. Their confessions carry consequences. Math and the learner overlap to create a region of conflict where self-awareness and social perception wrestle with each other. It is universally attributed to *"something to do with math."*

My teaching naturally pivoted towards removing as many impediments as possible. It took years of exposure and struggle to remove what lay scattered everywhere, from pebbles to boulders, strewn across hidden pathways, blocking them. Removing the obstacles and cutting through the thickets, exposed roads never travelled, routes never charted. Before me and my students, appeared vague outlines of learning pathways receding into the distance as far as the mind's eye could see. Together we took this road-not-travelled for the first time, and discovered ways to learn better, faster and with minimal resistance.

With the boulders removed, it was easy to see the slopes, the forks, the twists and turns on the road. They displayed unique patterns for each kind of mathematical activity. Subsequently, six distinct types of mathematical activities began to take shape. These evolved into the Six Stages. My subsequent readings and clinical experiences confirm that an authentic understanding of how math learning takes place, is derived from the teacher's granular exploration and understanding of *why and how it does* ***not*** take place. Next, they proceed to identify the impediments and remove them to disclose seamless, natural pathways to math learning.

The Six Stages postulate those interconnected, interlocking pathways, shown in the next chapter. It does not include Stage 0 which is introduced in **Appendix A (Stage 1)** as *"Setting the Foundations."* Stage 0 serves as a prelude to The Six Stages.

IV. THE DEEP KNOWLEDGE SYSTEM (DKS)

Two kinds of Deep Knowledge Systems (DKS) are occasionally mentioned throughout the Six Stages. For more on its conception and development, please refer to **Appendix A (Stage 1)**. It is explained in brief as follows:

Deep Knowledge System A:

This system generates symbolic thinking. Symbols are encoded knowledge that distill meaning. They compact things and ideas that have been understood, and represent them in packed forms with the knowns locked inside them. Symbols are decoded using "keys", each with a 1-on-1 correspondence.

Infants display a latent understanding of the coding systems. They are able to encode objects and quantities, sounds and forms that predicates their future ability to manage and control symbolic thinking.

Deep Knowledge System B:

This system drives intent, a hidden urge manifested by wanting to do something that feels do-able. Upon attaining some fluency with their encoding and decoding process, infants display intentional behaviours that are driven by their need to understand tasks they perform physically, what they read, how they communicate what they understand, e.g. pointing at specific pictures and commenting on them as they develop their oral vocabulary and comprehension.

This ability helps them to explore the hidden content that is baked into mathematical rules algorithms. Assistive, inquiry-oriented pedagogy helps them to implant and extract numerical reasoning, impelled by an intent to store, know and understand.

The Six Stages build upon connections between encoding-decoding processes and intentional behaviour. We encode what we understand, which results in our decoding what we know. This process becomes automatic in mathematics where mathematical algorithms themselves become expressions of intent, motives and goals.

> *"Although it is necessary to infuse courses and curricula with modem content, what is even more important is to give students the tools they will need in order to use, understand, and even make mathematics that does not yet exist". (Cuoco and Goldenberg: "Habits of Mind," 1996)*

Today the construction, de-construction and reconstruction of reality derives from a consciousness of coding, i.e. encoding and decoding. In many ways what we see around us are coded services and products of mathematical thinking that lend themselves to decoding by users: producers, manufacturers and consumers alike.

Mathematics learning that demonstrates the encoding of symbols, in order to encode ideas and processes, offers learners the tools they will decode to apply what they already know. This lies at the heart of extending one's knowledge to solve problems. The success achieved during each of The Six Stages in this journey becomes a powerful and permanent deterrent to math anxiety.

Finally, this book (and the remaining 5 Stages that follow) is intended to be a practical as well as a theoretical resource for Master Teacher Trainers in Mathematics education. It is also intended for mathematics teachers who want to invite inquiry without fear, and provoke critical thinking with clarity, precision and a clear sense of direction.

It is hoped that this book will also serve the needs of researchers and instructional designers (curriculum and textbook developers) especially in the developing world. I also hope that all who conduct Math assessments, and clinical diagnostics related to math-learning difficulties such as dyscalculia will find the book helpful.

SHAD MOARIF

Woking, UK

November 3, 2022

THE SIX STAGES TO MATH MASTERY
– An Overview –

The Six Stages are organised so as to offer optimal pedagogical and learning advantages when teaching and learning math. They have been arranged in stages to reflect the evolving structure of mathematics as they correspond with increasing complexity. It is an educator/practitioner's reconstruction of mathematics as a school subject, viewed through the lenses of teaching and learning.

I. STAGE ZERO: Setting the Foundations, Appendix A (Stage 1)

Young pre-schoolers are presumed to be well past the rational-intuitive Approximate Number System in Stage 0. From age 6 years onwards they should be ready to learn the more advanced Natural Number System for Base 10, with their concept of 1-on-1 correspondence firmly anchored. Stage 1 follows the *Setting of Foundations* (Stage 0) where young learners wrap their linguistic membrane around numbers to understand numerical content.

For *older learners*, Stage 0 is the pre-learning stage for new middle and secondary level math topics that have yet to be introduced e.g. algebra and trigonometry. It assumes mastery over all prior mathematical knowledge needed to understand new math topics. New learners are expected to understand the significance of non-numerical symbols used in advanced secondary math topics.

Stage 1 is generic to all math topics. Regardless of grade or age level, all who learn to encode *math symbols* for the first time in Stage 1 will be able to encode *math concepts* in Stage 2.

STAGE 1: Encoding Mathematical Symbolisms
STAGE 2: Encoding Conceptual Understanding
STAGE 3: Processing Numbers
STAGE 4: Mathematical Operations
STAGE 5: Algorithmic Thinking
STAGE 6: Problem-Solving

STAGES 1 AND 2

Encoding Mathematical Symbolisms (Stage 0, Appendix), sets the foundations by introducing findings from neuro-cognitive research that explain the development of number sense from early infancy to age 5. Infants' understanding of numbers, although restricted, grows quickly into an awareness of numerical content, associated with number sounds and symbols via the Approximate Number System (ANS). The ANS is bolstered in parallel by early language learning and it subsequently evolves into our Base 10 Natural Number System.

From age 6-7 upwards, children are shown the process of encoding the most common mathematical operations: $=$, $+$, $-$, $\times$, $\div$, $<$, and $>$. Learners participate in deriving these codes after being shown how they originated and why they look the way they do.

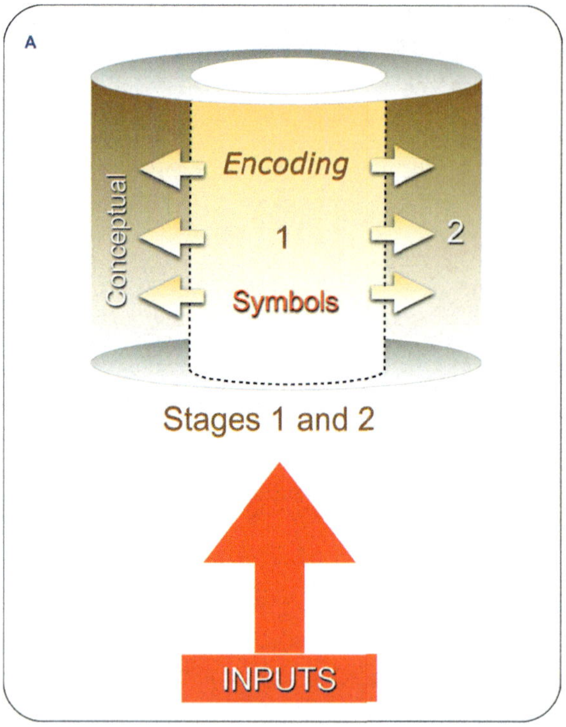

Stage 1 explains how we encode the following symbolisms. Mathematical meanings are compacted and converted into symbols, for easy manipulation of abstract ideas:

Symbolism 1: *Developing Symbolic Representation*
Symbolism 2: *Orientation and Regrouping*
Symbolism 3: *The Equality Symbol*
Symbolism 4: *1-to-1 Correspondence*
Symbolism 5: *Judging the Numerical Size of Quantities*
Symbolism 6: *The Four Mathematical Operation Symbols (+, −, ×, ÷)*
Symbolism 7: *Fractions*
Symbolism 8: *Functions*

In the image below, Stage 1 is shown inside the inner core (in the lighter colour) enveloped by an outer core (darker coloured) encasing Stage 2. The knowledge of math symbols in Stage 1 percolates through the porous membrane of the inner core (shown by outgoing arrows on each side) into the larger outer core to germinate a deep understanding of mathematical concepts covered in Stage 2:

In Stage 2, *Encoding Conceptual Understanding*, students graphically unravel the conceptual understanding of mathematical concepts through the use of Stage 1 math symbols e.g. one cannot understand multiplication if one is not familiar with the +, = and × signs; nor division, without the math symbols =, − and ÷.

The following topics are covered in Stage 2:

1. Encoding Long Multiplication
   - Multiplying Teen numbers with a Single Digit Number
   - Multiplying Teen Numbers by Teen Numbers
   - Multiplying-Ty Numbers by-Ty Numbers
2. Encoding the Simple Division Operation
   - Encoding the Long Division Concept
   - Encoding the Long Division Operation
   - Encoding Division as Equal Grouping
3. Encoding Properties and Behaviours of a Circle
4. Encoding Fractions as Part of a Group of Multiple Units — A & B
5. Encoding the Division-Fraction Connection
6. Encoding the Concept of Ratio
7. Encoding the Concept of Slope in Geometry
8. Encoding Decimal Fractions as Decimal Numbers
9. Encoding Percentage
10. Encoding Long Multiplication

As their understanding widens in scope, math symbols help articulate their understanding through tight, compact mathematical statements. Both experiences of encoding (Stages 1, and 2) enable instant de-coding for meaning upon sight.

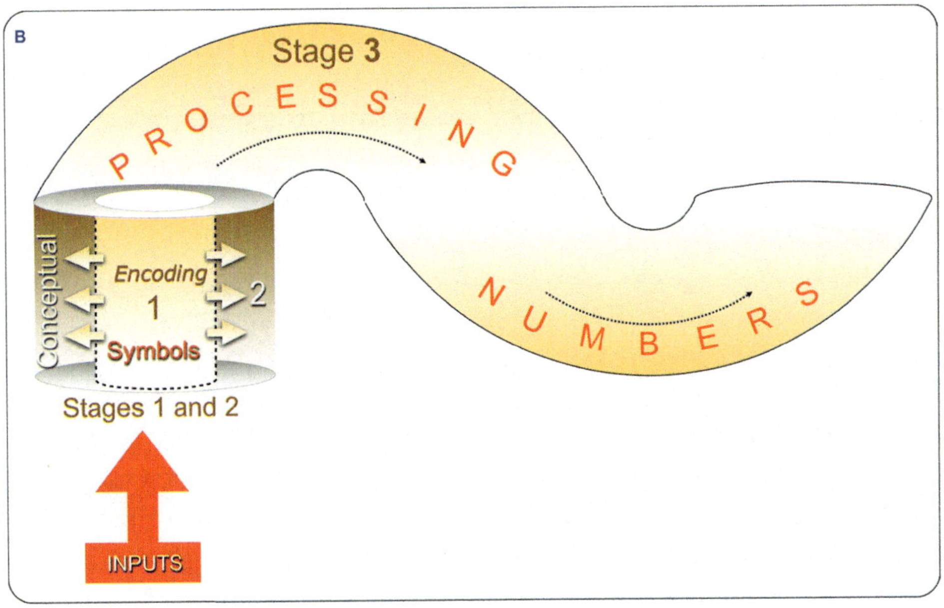

STAGE 3

Stage 3 *Processing Numbers*, is shown above in the form of a "flow". Learners bring with them the load of a growing traffic of numbers, pouring out of Stages 1 and 2. They require speedy and accurate processing just as heavy traffic requires traffic-flow planning to pre-empt logjams in the foreseeable future.

Stage 2 concepts such as multiplication and division switch gears and turn into higher-order operations (in Stage 4). These have to be conducted with speed, accuracy and fluency, to achieve mastery. Numbers are processed sequentially and simultaneously at certain thresholds of speed to prevent the operational processes from breaking down. It is like balancing on a bicycle only when it moves at a certain minimal speed, or a plane capable of liftoff at a certain ground-speed. In that respect, Stage 3 serves as a runway. Learners achieve sufficient computational speeds for lift-off into the abstract world of mathematical operations awaiting them in Stage 4.

Increasing processing and computational speeds frees up the energy and mental space needed to pilot more complex, higher level executive tasks in math. Number processing serves as a *cognitive lubricant* that makes executive decision-making smooth and adaptive.

The exercises in Stage 3 are designed to speed up number-processing (linear and simultaneous 2-track processing), mental computation and multiplication tables. Stage 3 also introduces topics that are difficult to visualise but easy to understand using simple numerical reasoning. Numbers are re-assembled and re-purposed to generate entirely new mathematical concepts that are almost entirely numerical and abstract. Stage 3 demonstrates how numbers can be processed and reformulated to create unique mathematical meaning with new topic labels. Learners find number-processing meaningful when they are shown how useful and labour-saving it can be in learning higher-level math. The new topics begin from No. 5 in the list below:

1. Reading large numbers correctly
2. Swift and accurate mental calculations, at least with double digits.
   (What is 36 + 25? Answer in 5 seconds or less, without calculating on paper).
3. Mastery in Times Tables

4. Simultaneous-parallel number-processing
5. Assembling and Processing:
   A. Factors: Prime, and GCF
   B. Multiples: LCM
   C. Square Numbers and their Roots (or Square Roots)
   D. Exponents.
6. Processing Place Values in Multiplication
7. Processing Numbers in Fractions:
   A. Processing Fractions for Standard Part-Whole Relationships
   B. From Improper to Mixed Fractions
   C. From Mixed to Improper Fractions
   D. Comparing LIKE Fractions
   E. Comparing UNLIKE Fractions
8. Processing Decimal Numbers

STAGES 4 AND 5

Stage 3 *number processing* remains intrinsic and flows through the remaining stages like a river through arid land, turning them green and fertile. Stage 4, is shown in Frame C above, as the second inner core.

Mathematical Operations are used to obtain a broader, in-depth understanding of higher-level math topics. They turn like cogs in complex machines, turning smoothly with precision. At this stage aspects of mathematical concepts require movement to be understood and operations generate such movements. As their confidence and skill with number-processing increase, learners begin to think and reason with numbers and develop a keen mathematical readiness for future problem-solving. The Topics covered in Stage 4 are:

1. The Order of Operations (BEDMAS)
2. The Concept and Use of Negative Numbers
3. Concept of Equivalence in Framing Equations as mathematical Operations
   * Add-Subtract Equations
   * Multiply-Divide Equation
   * Combinations.
4. Averages, Mean and Median
5. Making Equal Fractions
   * Comparing UNLIKE Fractions
   * Using Equal Fractions
6. Comparing Decimal Fractions
7. Fraction of Groups
8. Changing Quantities by a Fraction
9. Using mathematical Algorithms

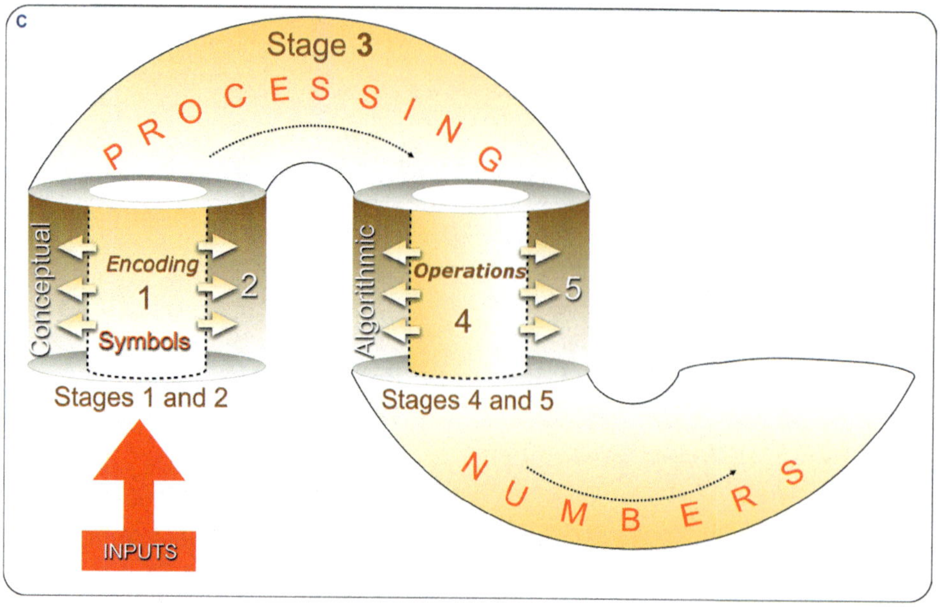

Stage 5, *Algorithmic Thinking*, is shown as the second outer core in the image. Learners begin to record specific mathematical steps that express numerical and conceptual reasoning when solving a mathematical problem. In a sense, the broad scatter of mathematical operations in Stage 4 reduces to an exact sequence of mathematical operations that *cracks the code*, to find the solution. The arrows on either side suggest free-flowing exchanges between the two stages. From Stage 4, learners' knowledge of operations *inform* Stage 5. A fine, invisible line is drawn around a set of carefully curated operations as their choice of steps leading up to an algorithm.

Stage 5 contains topics that need a very short conceptual run-up (area, perimeter, volumes) to be understood conceptually. Stage 5 also explains the mechanics of changing the subject of an equation, the making of formulas, and the significance of prescribing carefully sequenced procedures to generate new concepts such as trigonometric ratios and Pythagoras' theorem.

Topics covered in Stage 5 are:

1. What are Algorithms?
2. Personal Heuristics
3. Prefabricated Algorithm Templates
4. Algorithmic Templates in Multiplication and Division
5. Algorithmic Thinking
6. Algorithm or Formula?
7. Area and Units of Measurement
8. Perimeter
9. Area of Circles
10. Volume of Prisms
11. Surface Areas

STAGE 6

Stage 6, *Problem Solving*, begins by introducing a cognitive framework for problem-solving. This Stage is the outermost sphere containing a very large space. In Frame D below, it is shown as the final Output core, in green. In this stage learners assimilate various approaches to problem-solving in different topics. This stage dwells extensively on fractions, because they consolidate

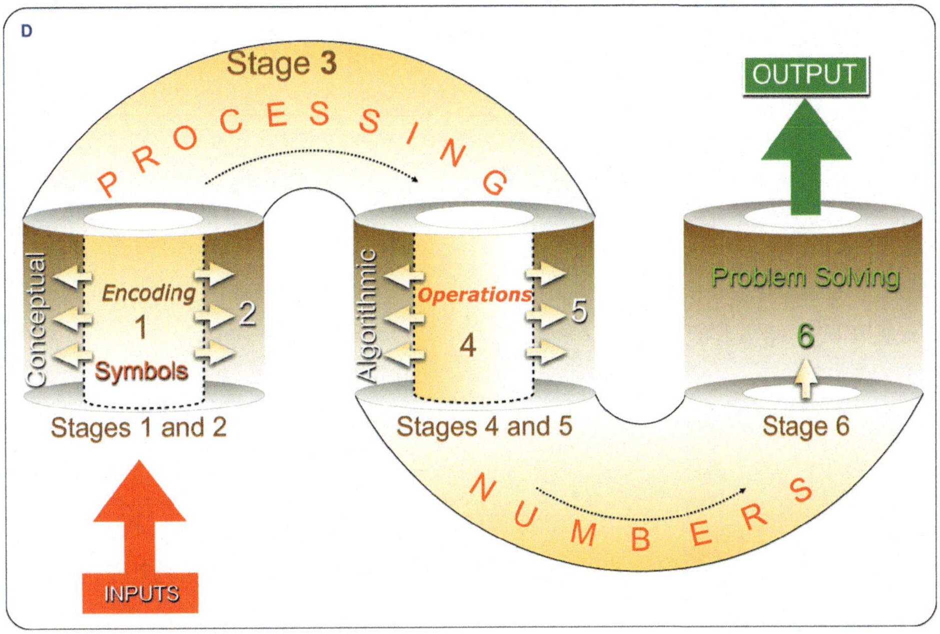

many math concepts learned throughout the preceding stages. Other selected topics are related to fractions since they are derived from it, except for equations, which straddles middle-secondary school.

Learners begin to incorporate their knowledge of the math concepts gleaned from the preceding five stages by using them purposefully. Unbundling and tackling problems help learners test, then hone their cumulative skills and expertise selectively. They learn to access their memory archives and sift through extraneous numerical noises to find what they are looking for to solve a problem. By now, their robust use of visual, verbal, numerical and abstract reasoning enables their fluent recall and retrieval. The math topics cover very diverse approaches and strategies that are unveiled graphically, incrementally, in steps and stages.

Topics:

1. Fractions
2. Percentage
3. Profit and Loss
4. Equations

STAGE 2

Encoding Conceptual Understanding

The first most comprehensive resource for Mathematics teacher-trainers and Teachers

This is the second in a 6-parts series

STAGE 2 – Introduction

Concept (Latin concipere "to take in and hold; become pregnant") means to give birth to an idea conceived in the mind. It's similar to the process of birth, which starts from cross-fertilisation. For example, humans once took the knowledge of the hardness and durability of a tree trunk and cross-fertilised it with the knowledge of rolling boulders down slopes to produce a new idea: rollers. The roller is the product of a concept. It seems, therefore, that our perception of reality splits readily into two states. When the mind imagines the trunk to be rollers, it separates the outer (tree) and the inner (concept of rollers). Likewise, in mathematics, conceptualising is a way of imagining. Our mind can reach beyond outer phenomena (quantity of things) and interface with its inner state to produce mathematical concepts that can be put to use.

A. Precognition

Stage 1 introduced findings from neuro-cognitive research that confirm the presence of two nascent abilities in infants:

A) *Encoding Ability*: Newborn babies come equipped with mysterious precognition engines that work like knowledge acquisition systems. These systems can be triggered to provoke cross-modal encoding and decoding of auditory and visual stimuli. This ability was tested for matching quantities and is manifested as early as a day or two after birth.

For language, Noam Chomsky noted that infants, without any formal assistance, acquire untaught rules of spoken language, its grammar and syntax, with remarkable accuracy, ease, and fluency, within 4-5 years of their birth.

It seems, therefore, that children are born with automatic knowledge-acquisition engines humming inside their brains that can encode language vaguely, and numbers approximately, before they are exposed to their first formal learning experiences.

B) *Intentional Behaviour:* Infants also display intentional behaviour when they react with their environment while being able to anticipate a future state of being. Their knowledge-acquisition systems are triggered to provoke change, to move a state from what once was to what will be.

Often, when driven by sheer curiosity, babies crawl through social barriers with ease, but as soon as they start to walk, they bump into social cues appearing as do's and don'ts encoded by parents and adults. They decode these approve-disapprove signals as their curiosity draws them into a journey of learning binary social prompts that symbolise yes/no, allowed/not allowed, and so on. Not long after, they learn to express their own intent symbolically by modelling their parent's physical gestures, oral and facial expressions.

Children's curiosity is aroused by a need to know what makes things and behaviours change from one state to another. They encode their intentions, motives, and goals by following a familiar intention-motive-goal cycle:

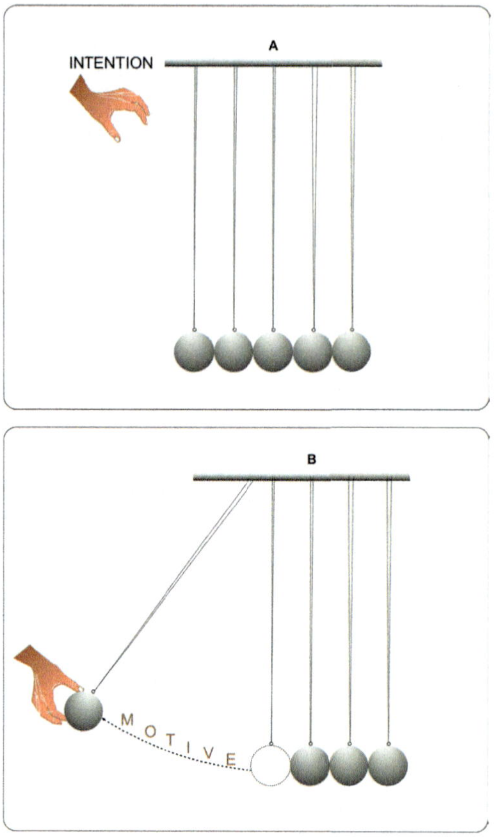

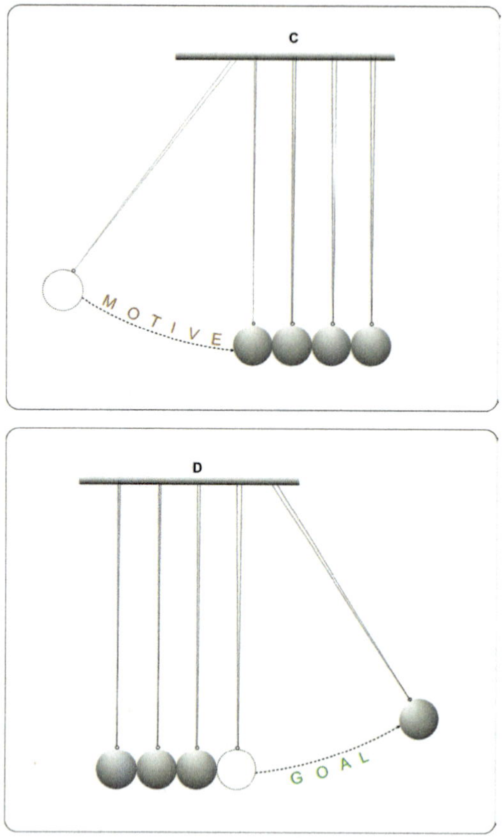

As learners, a child's conceptual development depends heavily upon analysing, rehearsing, and recalling the process. If understood well, the change of status from A to D in the graphic above can be conceptually encoded like a well-cut key. It can be used to unlock the same process mentally, over and over again. When repeated experiences validate what children know to be true, they move on to augment their repertoire of experiences and discover new areas to test their intended activity.

During formative assessments, two of the best questions to ask are those that respect children's intention: *What do you want to do now?* and *What would you like to do next?* These questions are less intimidating than: *What should you do now?* or *What happens next?* because they anticipate an adherence to rules. They are accepted only after their intention has been explored with timely prods of reasoning (*Why?*).

B. Encoding Understanding in terms of Nature and Nurture

Nature: What we understand to be innate human "*nature*" appears to correspond closely with knowledge acquisition engines. They accelerate during children's exploratory activities. In this context, human *nature* behaves like a sophisticated receptacle that curates raw sensory inputs (*"Ugh!! I need to push harder to slide myself from here to there!"*) and turns them into learning. Much of it gets distilled into basic concepts to be stored in their long-term memory for future retrieval. They anticipate future germination.

In high school physics, we learn that "Work *done is the product of the force-strength and the distance travelled*". In other words, work is a product of the cross-pollination between energy spent and distance moved. This statement feels almost intuitive, i.e., *we measure work in terms of the amount of energy spent in moving a certain distance*. We experienced this when we slid on the floor upon our haunches, or crawled on all fours, and then learned to walk. Today we know better than ever before how new activities of the present revive memories of past experiences and evoke something that feels remotely familiar but immediately meaningful. Perhaps this is one way of experiencing cognitive resonance.

It is in our nature to encode concepts numerically and linguistically. As a consequence, much of early learning is a measure of children's conceptual development. It takes time, effort, and practice before what is *understood* and *learned* emerge as products of *manifested know*ledge, as in progressing from rollers to wheels.

The knowledge progression is:

understand ⇨ learn ⇨ know

Nurture: In this context, *nurture* comprises all the elements that are harnessed to foster *nature*. It provides the scaffolding that supports *nature*. Without it, *nature* would remain largely unmanifested. The infant's knowledge-acquisition engine (*nature*) receives elements of learning that cohere in unknown ways to become encoded concepts. Without them, we would be hard-pressed to explain what we understand except through gestures and drawings. Driven by intent and stirred by curiosity, children keep increasing their capacity to encode more concepts simply by consuming what *nurture* provides:

(a) nourishment (air, food, water, etc.) within our social ecosystem.
(b) informal (play) learning.
(c) formal (non-coercive) learning.

Curiosity-inspired behaviours, when satisfied, have provoked ideas since the dawn of civilization, ideas that design the future with elements from the present, such as vehicles from wheels:

At the other end of the encoding spectrum lies anxiety. It is aroused when there are psycho-social hindrances in exercising intentional behaviour, cultural restraints in formulating motives, and unconscious impediments in articulating goals.

Any disconnect between the growing child's nature and nurture, caused by disparities in the social ecosystem, risks setting off cognitive dissonance in the workings of both. A punitive and iniquitous social system breeds symptoms of dysfunction in the ability to receive learning or in the ability to deliver learning experiences. In extreme cases, it may even risk stunting intellectual growth temporarily. Curiosity fettered by anxiety can weaken the arousal of intent. It inhibits active learning. By the same token, however, moderate levels of anxiety serve as shock-and-pain absorbers, a first line of defence. If managed intelligently and creatively, it can disable the consequences of inequity from damaging the entire cognitive system. Therefore, the temporary disabling allows time for nature and nurture to recalibrate their relationship in new ways, restore their cognitive resonance, and reconnect so that healthy intentional behaviours may recommence.

C. Encoding Conceptual Understanding

Conceptualisation can be a mental representation of the intended actions to be taken. When envisioning the design of a garden, many gardeners resort to imagination that brings to the fore all they like and dislike. They curate different arrangements of plants, pots, and borders as doodles on paper until the most pleasing design is conceived for planning purposes. This is followed by elaborate sketches and further modifications until a vision is finalised for implementation. In Stage 2, mathematical understanding is *mapped* out conceptually. They are *planned*, using numbers and symbols, and finally recorded for subsequent use.

Stage 1 learners encode mainly mathematical operational symbols that contain meaning and provoke behaviour. It is a bit like what we do when we see the sign:

They provoke a significant change in our behaviour, but only for a short duration. Children learn math symbols like single words whose meanings are demonstrated in their use in brief sentences but not much more.

In Stage 2, they learn to encode an entire mathematical concept as processes, from beginning to end, using symbols that are now familiar to them. These are combined with new mathematical symbols that by themselves have no meaning:

Concepts are easy to understand because they are already embedded in precognition. The roundness of a rubber ring is *known* generically to most 6-year-olds. By contrast, its *mathematical conceptualisation* delves into specific behaviours (roll, bounce, cover a distance when rolled, etc.) unique to roundness. Its mathematical abstraction as a shape, "circle" or "sphere", introduces components that are related to each other (e.g., the outer boundary or the *circumference* is approximately *3 times the length of its diameter*). This is not difficult to understand, especially when explored as demonstrable truths. Older learners get it within minutes via drawings on the board and using a piece of string and a measuring tape. Nevertheless, the curious learner will still be piqued by the need to understand the teacher's intent. *"So what? Why do we need to know this?"*

Invariably, a narrative is needed, a story that demonstrates the importance of *"knowing this"*. Teachers often begin by tapping into the latent curiosity aroused among interested learners. Master teachers can't help giving that curiosity a timely prune that clips one fork of curiosity, keeping the other growing in the right direction, i.e., towards the build-up of a mathematical concept.

A large rubber ring held up with both hands, like a steering wheel, can tease out conceptual thinking:

(a) rotating the wheel in space around a fixed centre produces only rotational movement. Why does it not move forward? What makes it move forward when rotated? (*Contact* with the floor, *resistance, friction.*)

(b) When placed on the floor or the table, then turned, it moves forward. What changed? (*Its position.*) What occurred? *(It moved a certain distance.)* When rotated upon a vertical axis through the centre, why does it not move forward?

(c) It makes 1 turn slowly, followed by another, equally slowly. What is the connection between how many times it turned and the distance it moved? *(Two full turns = twice the distance moved, and so on.)*

(d) Can one predict... no, estimate... no, calculate... yes, *calculate* the distance a wheel moves forward if it turns 15 times?

(e) What does one need to know to calculate this way? (*Find the length of the "rim" with a string...*)

(f) How can one know this length without using a string?

Inquiry lays down pathways to conceptual understanding that suggest the *mathematical way*. Inquiry leads to the conceptual understanding of circles such as: *"the distance a wheel moves in a single turn is roughly 3 times its width (diameter)"*. It can replace the vagaries of speculation with the exactitude of calculation. All who aspire for mastery in Mathematics want to migrate from *"I think..."* to *"I know"*. Cognitive gratification is pleasurable, empowering, and anxiety-dispelling. It helps build self-confidence.

In the pursuit of conceptual understanding, learners *follow target behaviours* (e.g., of a circle) with curiosity and interest, until something unexpected happens. It is like watching a paper boat floating on calm waters until a real boat comes along. When the circle rolls forward as a wheel, the hidden relationships between its various components come alive. They can be demonstrated. It gets easier to arouse students' curiosity about the connection between the circle's different components: the center, circumference, radius and diameter. Suddenly the circle is perceived as a simple, unpretentious entity, as un-selfconscious of its hidden power to arouse the human mind, as the flower, to stir the human heart.

A symbolic understanding of a physical reality made abstract is like a child imagining the television to contain tiny humans performing inside a "box" which has mysterious instruments and tools that make images behave like humans. Not long after, the "box" becomes an abstract entity that can be represented by a square or rectangle. It contains mysterious hidden powers. Likewise, the circle contains hidden aspects that can be harnessed intellectually to understand and control change from an initial state to a final (intended) state.

The process of learning Math in Stage 2 shows how to articulate what is understood in a coded form, one that embeds intent. To understand and know what the encoded form, $C = 2\pi R$ *means*, helps to anticipate and understand (a) the rotational speeds (RPMs or Revolutions per minute) of different-sized spokes in gears and (b) the ways they can be manipulated in order to make a bike to behave differently. This can be done by applying the numerical reasoning that is stitched into "rules" (often designed as algorithms).

Learners use numerical reasoning to join together math symbols in a meaningful way, as in $2 \times \pi \times R$, just as words are joined to make meaningful sentences. Expressing simple mathematical facts is not the same as explaining a mathematical concept, e.g., $4 = 4$ is a fact. However:

$$3 \times 8 = 8 + 8 + 8$$

and

$$8^3 = 8 \times 8 \times 8$$

suggest mathematical concepts. In Stage 2 learners draw heavily upon the use of reasoning and logical thinking. They learn to generate new strands of mathematical thinking. Indeed, combining their use of visual and numerical reasoning to encode math symbols in Stage 1 prepares them to use the same symbols to encode Conceptual Understanding in Stage 2.

Unfortunately, conventional math learning introduces mathematical concepts as a complex cobweb of terms and definitions that encode the known in ways that grow "curioser and curioser". The process of decoding them is like pulling teeth, and storing them in dark memory sheds as "rules". The rules themselves feel arbitrary, ambiguously explained, and difficult to remember. Until recently, much of mathematics was learned by rote, with faint glimmers of understanding and very little depth.

Such an approach makes the conceptual understanding of mathematics laborious and difficult right from the start. Years later, when in high school or college, some learners use their more mature and well-honed intelligence to decode the hidden meanings and significance of what they learned throughout their early schooling. Others distance themselves from Math because it evokes bitter memories of schooling, of a life plagued with chronic anxiety, fear, and self-doubt.

Such despairing experiences expose a broad and fertile mindscape for sowing popular myths such as, "learning and understanding mathematical concepts requires superior intellectual functioning. They are only for super-smart people!" Mathematics is still perceived as the abstract entity seated upon a throne on Mount Olympus, challenging the brightest among the bright, the strongest among the strong, the bravest among the brave to "dare cross the seven seas and seven heavens to come to me"!

Why would they? Most find it pretty thankless, even stupid, to exhaust themselves hacking through a dense jungle of linguistic, semantic definitions to get to the simplest and purest of math concepts. Often the concepts appear so exasperatingly obvious that learners begin to doubt their sanity: "What is it that I am not getting? Surely there must be more to it! Must be something else that only the smart ones can see!" These psychological setbacks constrict their conceptual understanding. It clogs their attempts to encode them. So when they fail to recall what they learned and understood they are flayed by anxiety. It is not that they find it hard to understand. It's just that it all feels so frustrating and complicated when they can't perform mathematical operations correctly. How can they, if they try to decode what they did not encode in the first place?

To rely on memorising rules gives learners a skewed understanding of what mathematics means: "to commit by heart, rules we don't understand. Only the smart ones do".

This is why it is so important for learners to participate actively in encoding their conceptual understanding into mathematical statements. As encoders of statements, they assume authorship of its mathematical form. They can be decoded easily to perform meaningful mathematical operations formally.

Of greatest value in Stage 2 is the growing ability of learners to sift through numerical "sounds" (cognitive noise) and settle upon only those that resonate cognitively. They discard those that trip cognitive dissonance (like plucking a string that is off tune) and begin to trust the "hunch that this feels right and that doesn't", e.g., mathematical statements feel right when written in a certain way, while others don't. If you skim over these three sentences, ask which one feels mathematically correct:

1) *"If a train has 16 carriages, then 5 identical trains will have 5 more carriages".*
2) *"If a train has 16 carriages, then 5 identical trains will have 64 more carriages".*
3) *"If a train has 16 carriages, then 5 identical trains will have 5 times more carriages".*

The correct mathematical statement(s) selected from the above makes one feel just right. Cognitive resonance is an important experience because often the best performers in sports and music dwell upon the memory of an emotion they feel each time they execute a skill with silky perfection. They seek to re-experience that emotion and reason emotionally while executing that skill. In Stage 2, the following conceptual processes are encoded in ways that, it is hoped, may penetrate your Deep Knowledge System:

1. Encoding Long Multiplication
    - Multiplying TeenNumbers with a Single Digit Number
    - Multiplying Teen Numbers by Teen Numbers
    - Multiplying -Ty Numbers by -Ty Numbers
2. Encoding the Simple Division Operation
    - Encoding the Long Division Concept
    - Encoding the Long Division Operation
    - Encoding Division as Equal Grouping
3. Encoding Properties and Behaviours of a Circle
4. Encoding Fractions as Part of a Group of Multiple Units — A & B
5. Encoding the Division-Fraction Connection
6. Encoding the Concept of Ratio
7. Encoding the Concept of Slope in Geometry
8. Encoding Decimal Fractions as Decimal Numbers
9. Encoding Percentage

SYMBOLISM 1

Encoding Long Multiplication

A. Multiplying Teen Numbers with Single Digits

Multiplication, as we saw in Chapter 2, *Encoding Math Symbolisms*, can be best visualised as an arrangement of arrays. These contain rows and columns of identical objects:

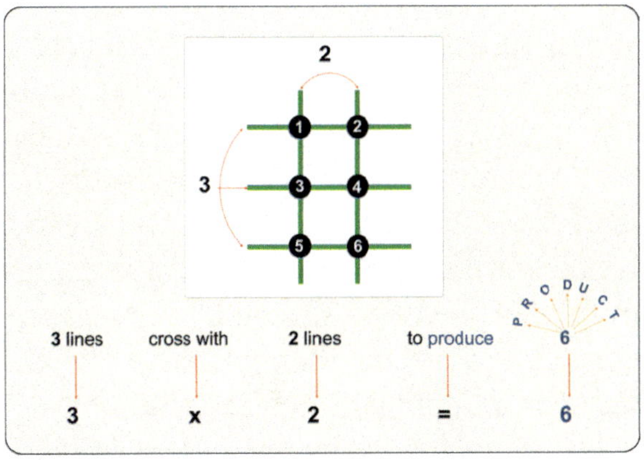

An obvious advantage of this is that ones' visual reasoning will confirm that 3 × 2 = 2 × 3. You can take any pair of rows and columns and switch them around but the number of items in the array (6) will remain unchanged. it is commonly known as the the Commutative Law. If one commutes via a route from A to B, and returns via the same route, then the distance covered from A to B will be the same as from B to A. Likewise, you can reverse the order of the numbers being multiplied. Their product will remain unchanged:

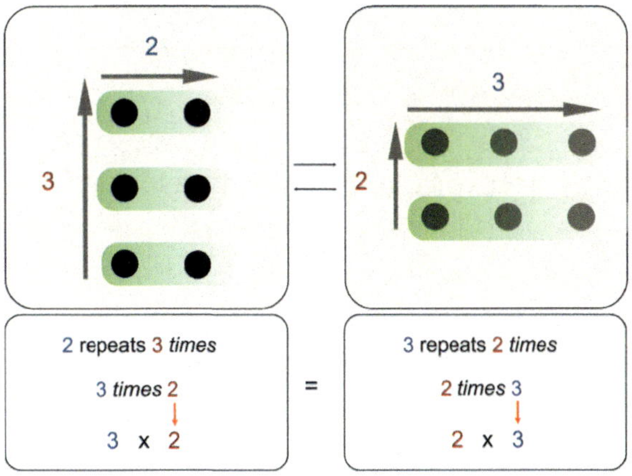

$$2 \times 3 \times 4 \times 5 = 3 \times 5 \times 2 \times 4$$

As a simple warm-up exercise, fill in the empty boxes below with numbers that demonstrate the Commutative Law:

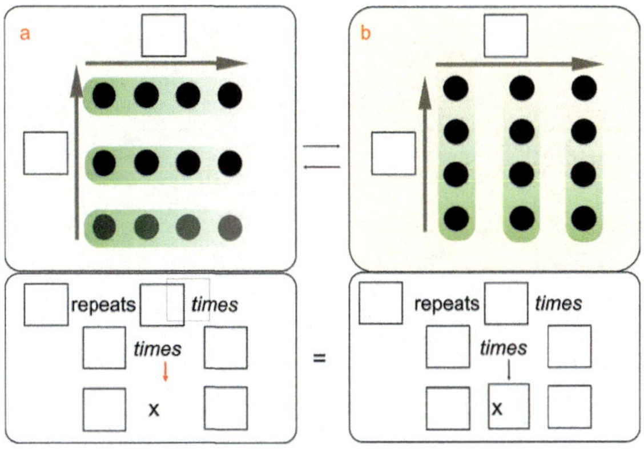

If the objects are tiles, then we can imagine multiplication to be an operation that entraps rectangular surfaces to define their sizes. Square tiles in particular serve as a standard measure of a surface's area. Consequently, the process for finding surface-areas (introduced much later) feels almost intuitive and resonates with the Deep Knowledge System:

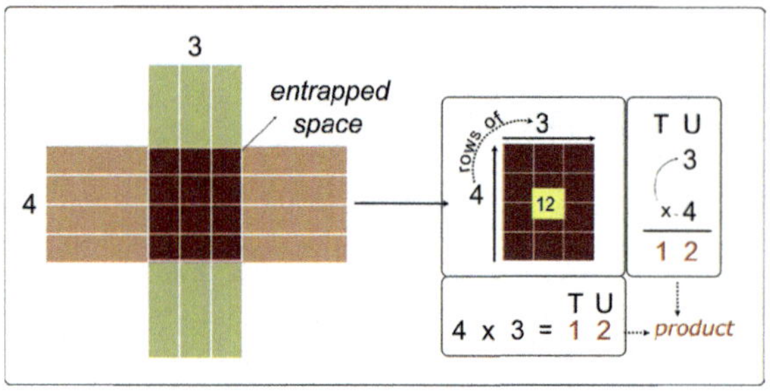

The intersecting spaces illustrated above, produce a measurable area or product. The product, 12, is a measure of the entrapped brown square tiles. Even better, we can show long multiplication to be a systematic process of construction. The multiplication below shows two separate constructions, 4 × 10 and 4 × 3:

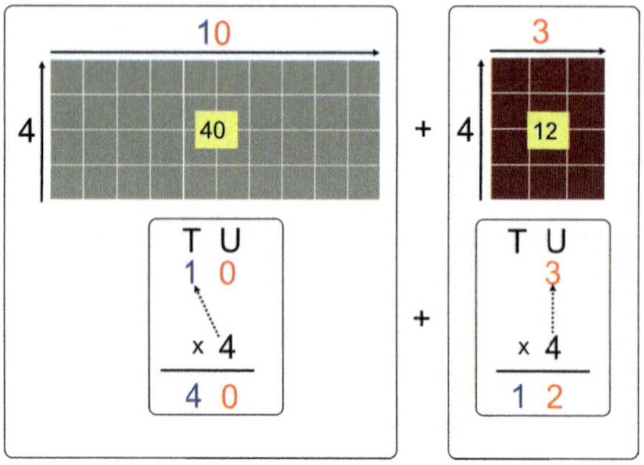

When the two are are joined together they appear as 4 × (10 + 3) or 4 × 13:

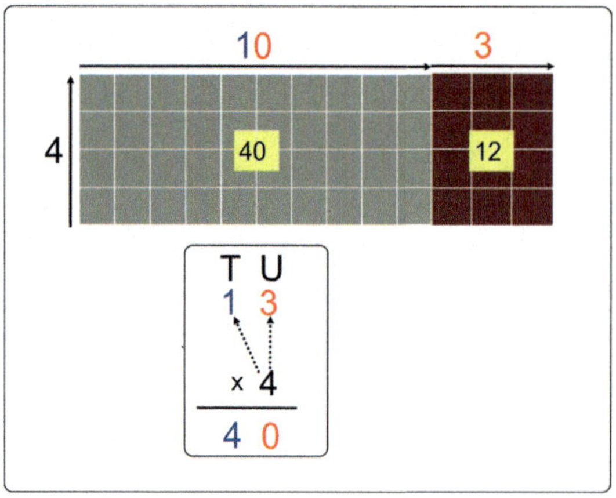

The vertical multiplication shown below is a basic representation of long multiplication using teen numbers multiplied by a singly digit. The most important principle to note here is the splitting of a double digit number like 13, into Tens and Units:

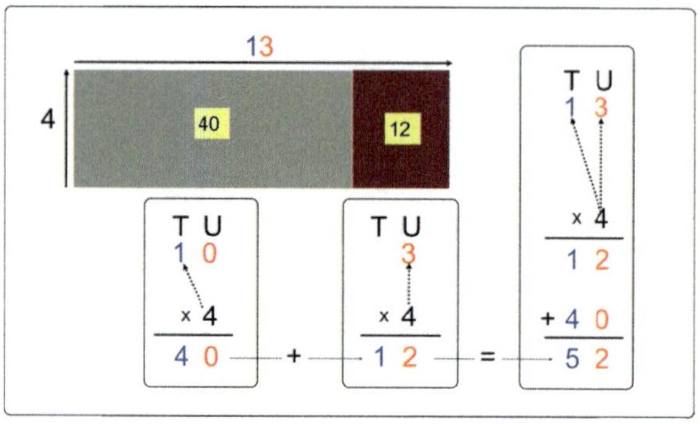

The product of 4 × 3 (=12) is added to that of 4 × 10 (= 40). The answer 40 + 12 (= 52) is the total number of tiles produced by multiplying 4 rows of 13 tiles or 4 times 13.

If you were to multiply 4 × 18, then 18 would be split horizontally into (10 + 8). The length of the longer rectangle would be 10, to represent the Tens component. The length of the shorter rectangle will always represent the unit component, like 8. The multiplier 4 will be shown by the vertical component. If the multiplier was 6, the vertical component would be 6 units long.

Now try 6 × 14 shown in (a) below. Fill in the empty boxes with numbers:

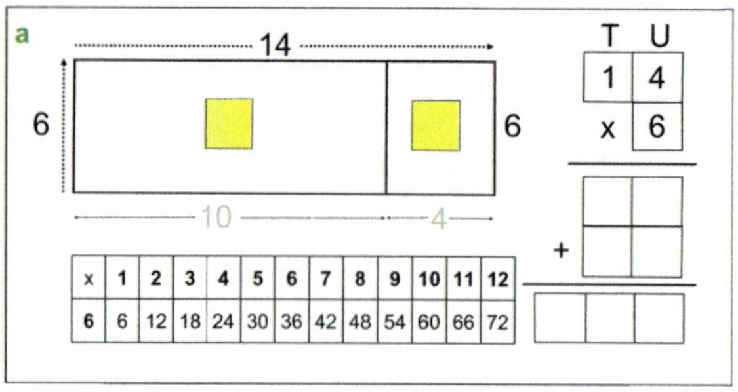

You can imagine the number 14 to be split in Tens and units as 10 + 4. Here are the 6 steps to follow:

1) Begin from right to left, taking the smaller rectangle first. The vertical 6 is the multiplier.

The joined length of both rectangles is 14. So the longer length should be 10, and the shorter length would be 4 tiles long.

2) What numbers go in the yellow squares? (Use the tables of 6). The product of each rectangle is printed in the yellow squares.
3) Copy the two products into the pairs of empty boxes just below the the long multiplication (right frame)
4) Add them both and you should get the 2-digit product, 60 + 24 = 84. A third answer box is provided in provided to practice with larger numbers. Now try this one entirely on your own:

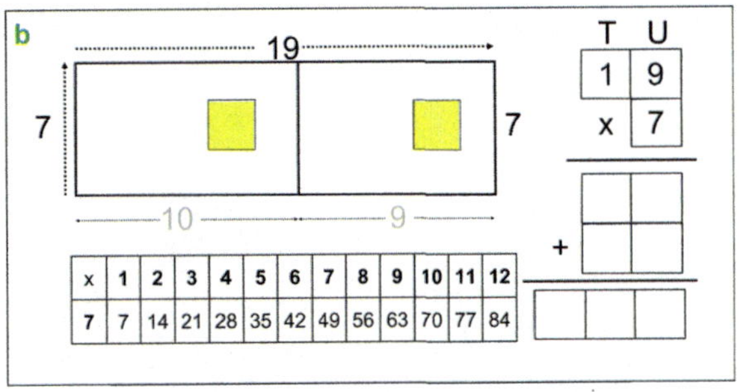

x	1	2	3	4	5	6	7	8	9	10	11	12
7	7	14	21	28	35	42	49	56	63	70	77	84

If you are already feeling tense and anxious, just put the book down, rest and and return to read it later later. Your confidence will increase only with practice, so here is a generic practice template for you to use:

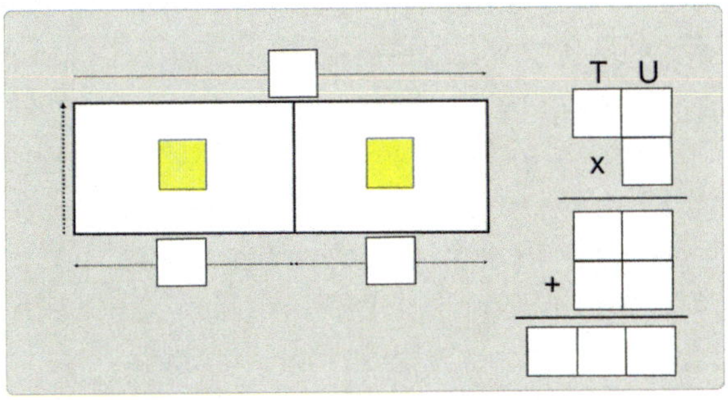

It shows the long and the short rectangle to represent the Tens and Units in any 2-digit teen-number of your choice. Don't fret over the sizes and proportion of the rectangle. Split your number into Tens (long rectangle) and Units (short rectangle). Then begin filling in all the boxes just as you did before. Use the multipliers provided below in the following times-tables:

multiplier

x	1	2	3	4	5	6	7	8	9	10	11	12
3	3	6	9	12	15	18	21	24	27	30	33	36

x	1	2	3	4	5	6	7	8	9	10	11	12
4	4	8	12	16	20	24	28	32	36	40	44	48

x	1	2	3	4	5	6	7	8	9	10	11	12
6	6	12	18	24	30	36	42	48	54	60	66	72

You can chose the height of the rectangle (the number of rows) to be 3, 4 or 6. As you do these, you will feel your anxiety dissipate. It is because when you start to know and understand something, you have power over it. When you don't, then the not-knowing and not-understanding has power over you. It is probably the most burdensome cause of anxiety.

B. Multiplying Teen Numbers by Teen Numbers

How do we multiply teen numbers where both have two digits? Let us take 14 × 16. We will break each teen number into Tens and Units as: 14 = 10 + 4 and 16 = 10 + 6. We now proceed to multiply: (10 + 4) × (10 + 6) as shown below. Here the vertical component is = 10 + 4 and the horizontal component is 10 + 6:

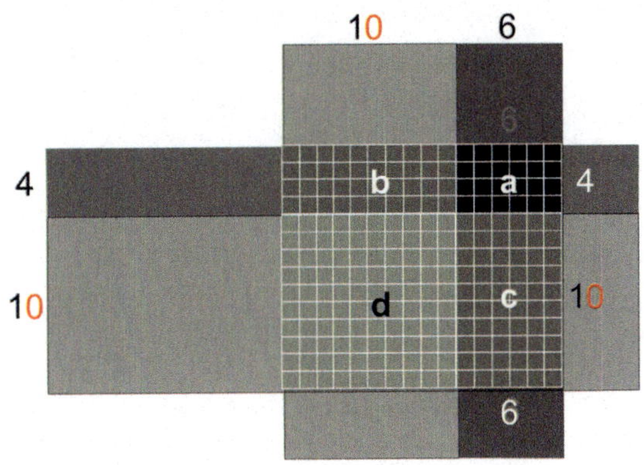

Clearly, the four entrapped spaces (a, b, c, and d) are represented by four distinct rectangles of different sizes, each containing the same-sized square tiles. These are shown separately below:

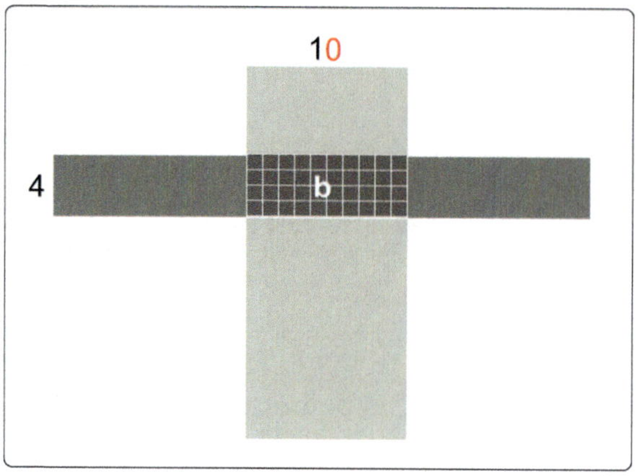

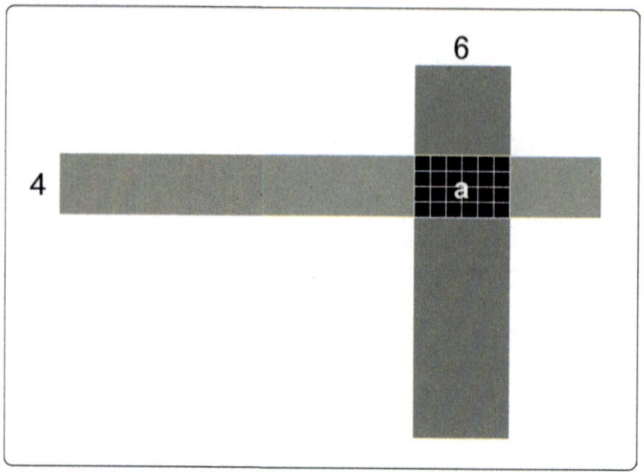

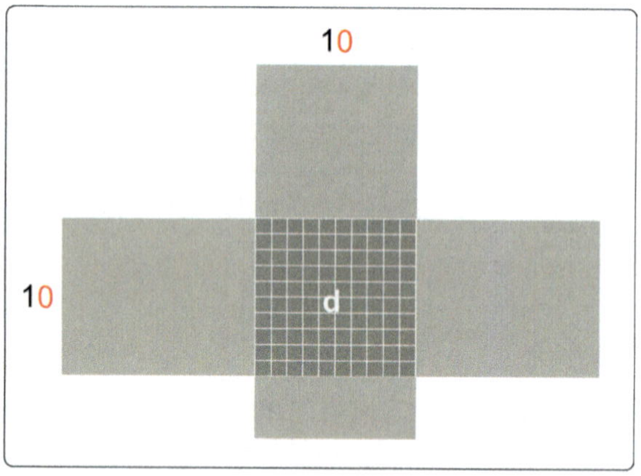

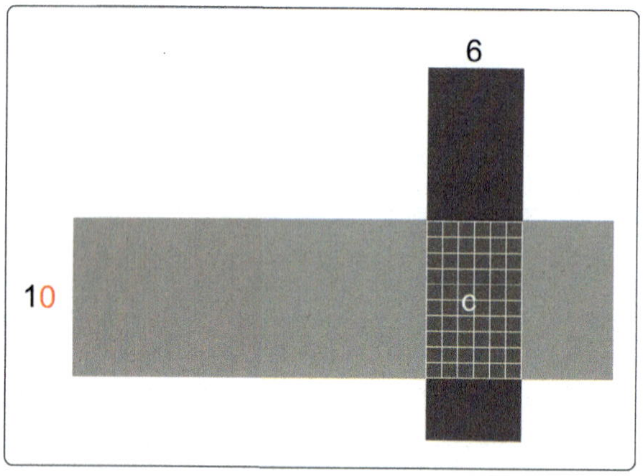

The four entrapped spaces contain the following products:

a. 4 × 6 = 24; **b**. 4 × 10 = 40
c. 10 × 6 = 60; **d**. 10 × 10 = 100

Below, the long multiplication is shown as resulting from the extraction of four multiplication steps. In a, 4 is multiplied by 6, then by 10. Next, 10 is multiplied by 6 and then by 10.

This is how multiplication of 14 × 16 brings together a set of four products a, b, c, d. We add them up to get the final product, 224, shown above.

Let us convert this into a Do It Yourself (DIY) exercise. The step-by-step guide for 14 × 16 will serve as a generic template for any pair of teen numbers to be multiplied (see p. 13).

Left Frame(fig. i): Make a rectangle. Mark off (with a small red line) the 10 (in 14), on the vertical side. The remaining portion of the line would automatically be 4.

Right Frame (fig. ii): First draw a straight line (green) parallel to the horizontal lines, as shown. Next mark off the 10 (in 16) with a tiny red line, on the horizontal side.

Left Frame (fig. iii): Draw a vertical line (green) from your red mark, to the opposite horizontal. So, the remaining portion will automatically be 6.

Right Figure (fig iv): Label your final diagram as shown. If you wish, you can colour each of the four inner rectangles a, b, c an d in different shades so they each stand out.

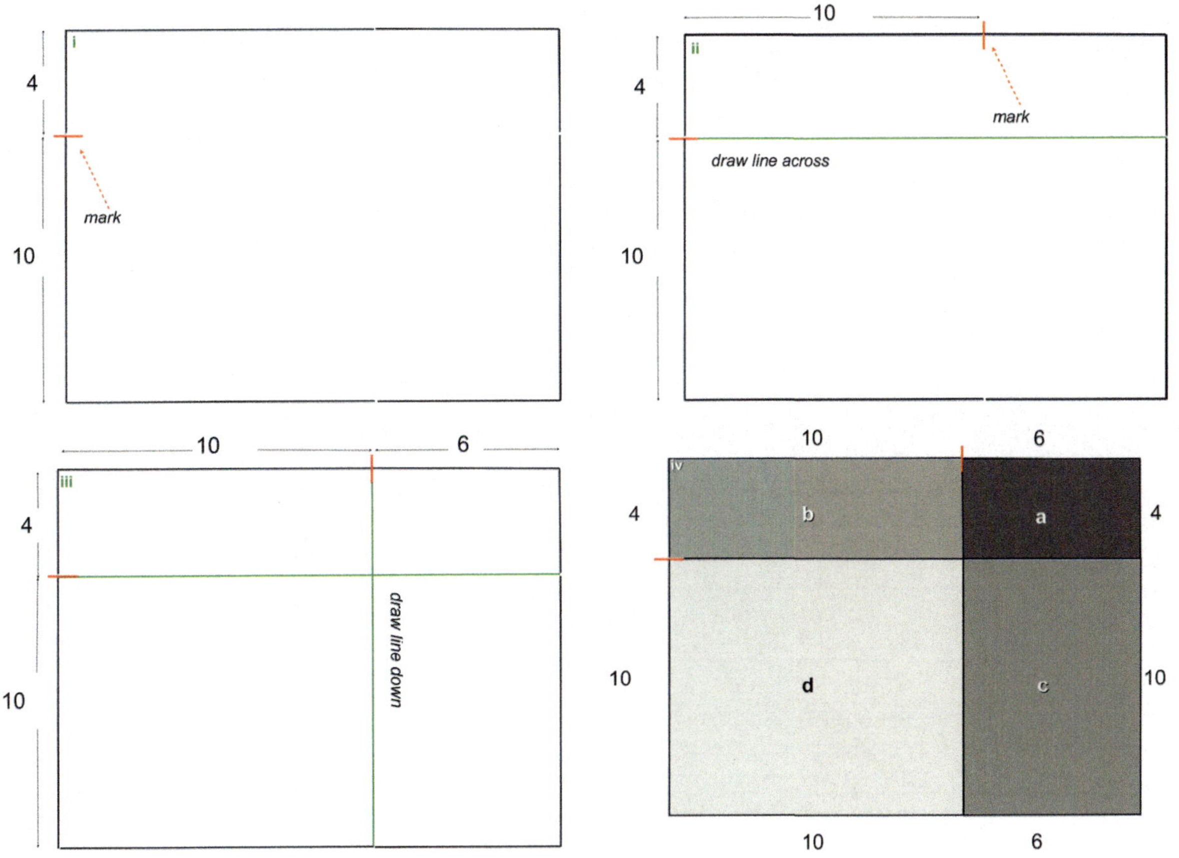

Here is how you find the four different products in each of the rectangles a, b, c and d:

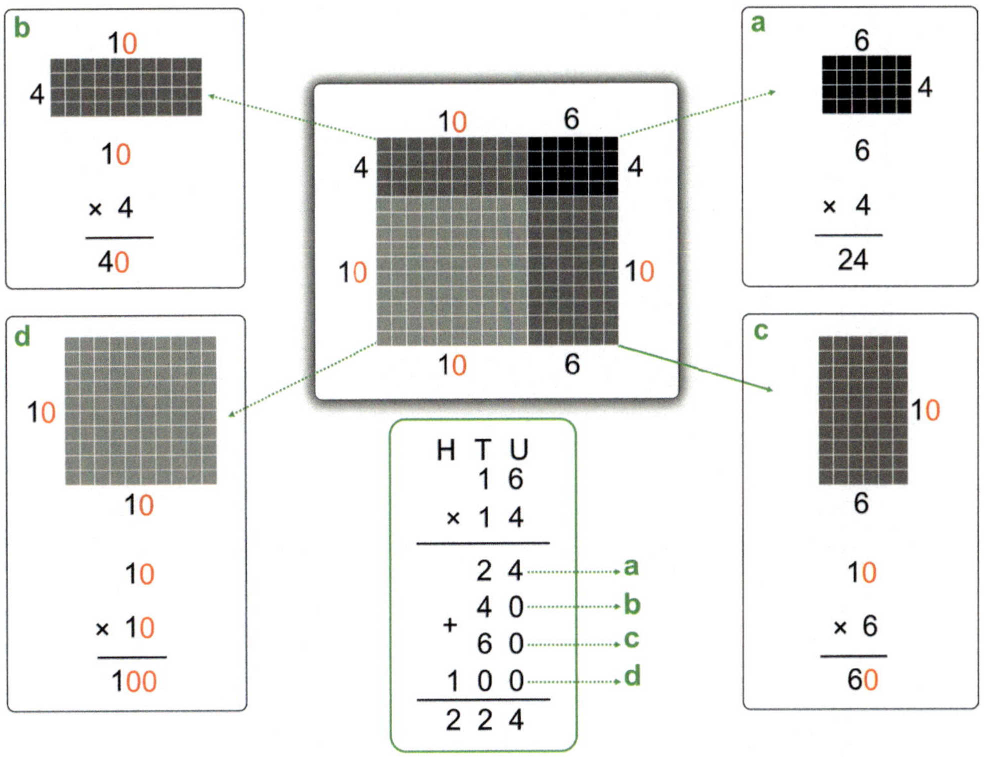

Now try doing these on your own:

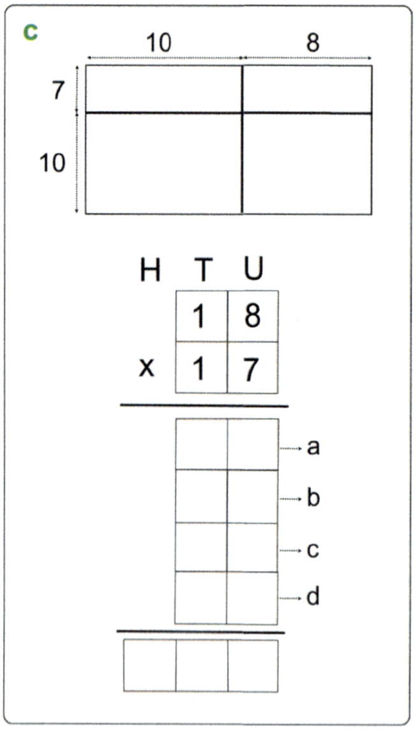

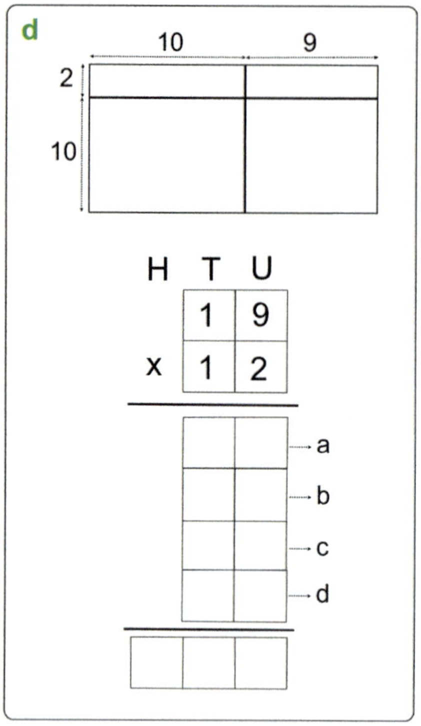

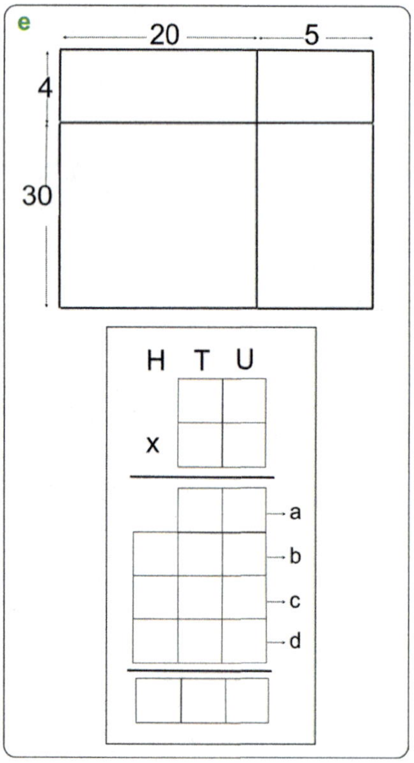

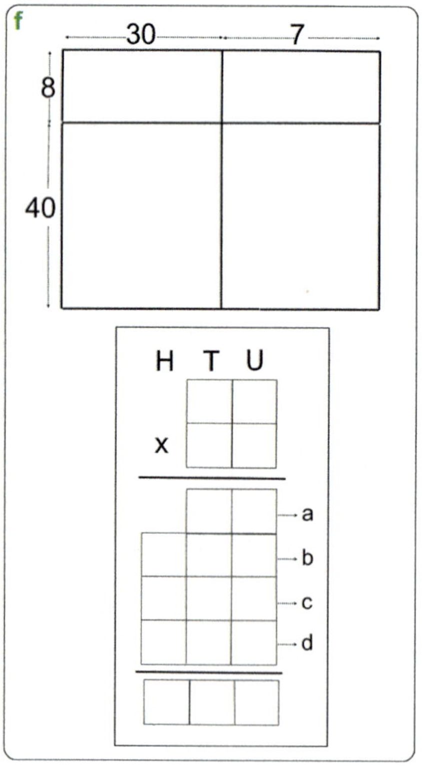

Do make up your own teen-pairs to multiply. It won't be long before they appear effortless.

C. Multiplying -Ty Numbers by -Ty Numbers

This means multiplying any pair of 2-digit numbers. To multiply 26 × 28 follow the same convention of finding the four products then adding them up. First break each number into Tens and Units. This time there will be 2 Tens (twenty) for each:

$$26 = 20 + 6$$
$$28 = 20 + 8$$

20 + 6 goes up along the vertical side, and 20 + 8 goes across along the horizontal side. Each one splits into two at 20. As before, their intersections produce four entrapped spaces (a, b, c, and d) as shown below:

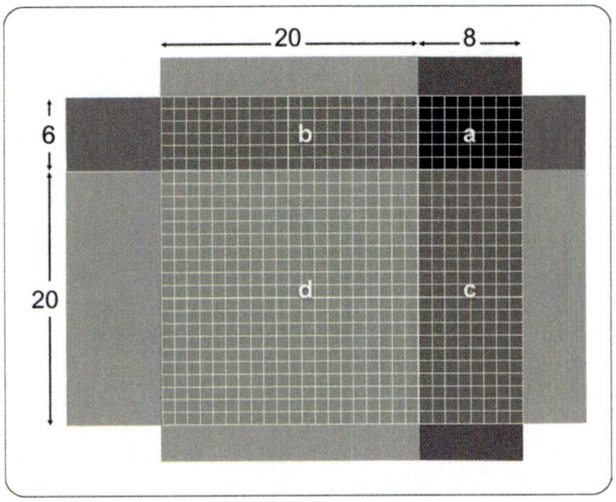

These are shown separately below:

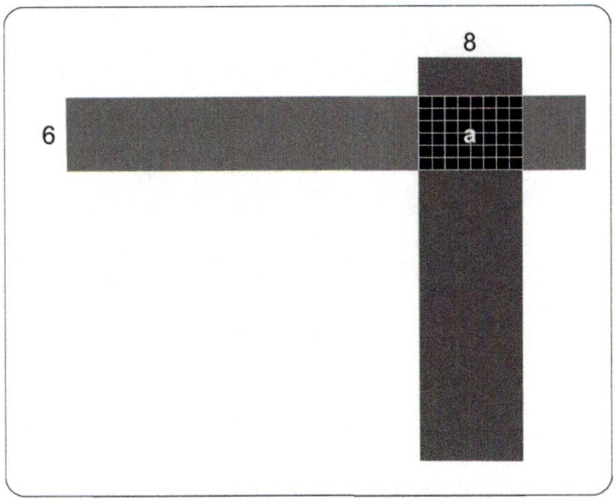

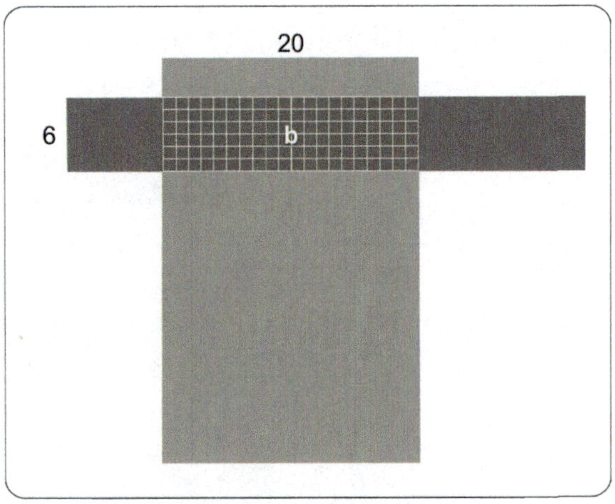

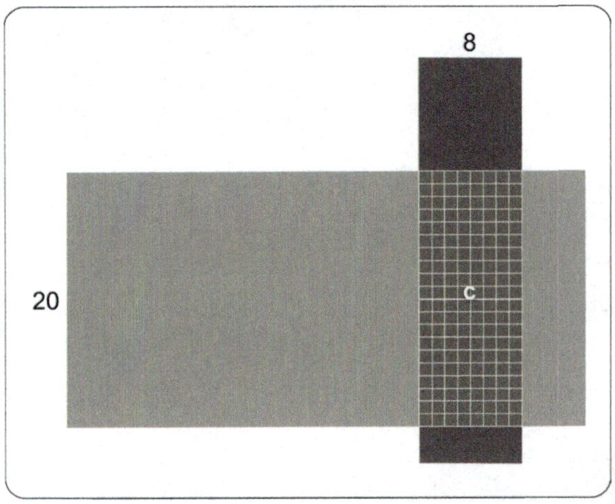

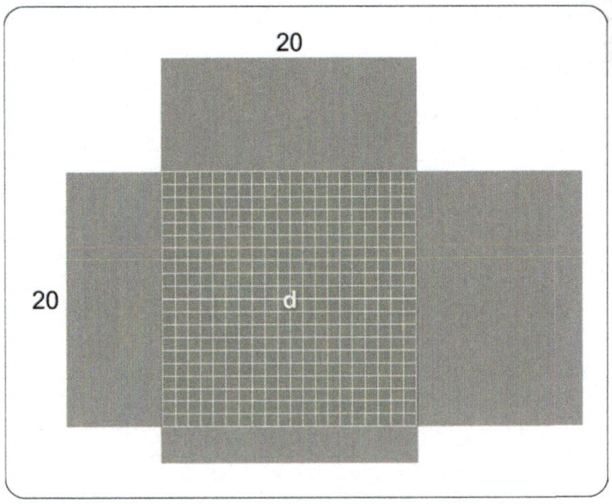

The four entrapped spaces contain the following products:

a. 6 × 8 = 48; **b**. 6 × 20 = 120
c. 20 × 8 = 160; **d**. 20 × 20 = 400

In the frame below, the 3 rectangles a, b, and c and a square, d in the middle, represent 4 multiplication operations. They are recorded numerically on the right as long multiplication. The final product is a sum of the four products: 48 + 120 +160 + 400.

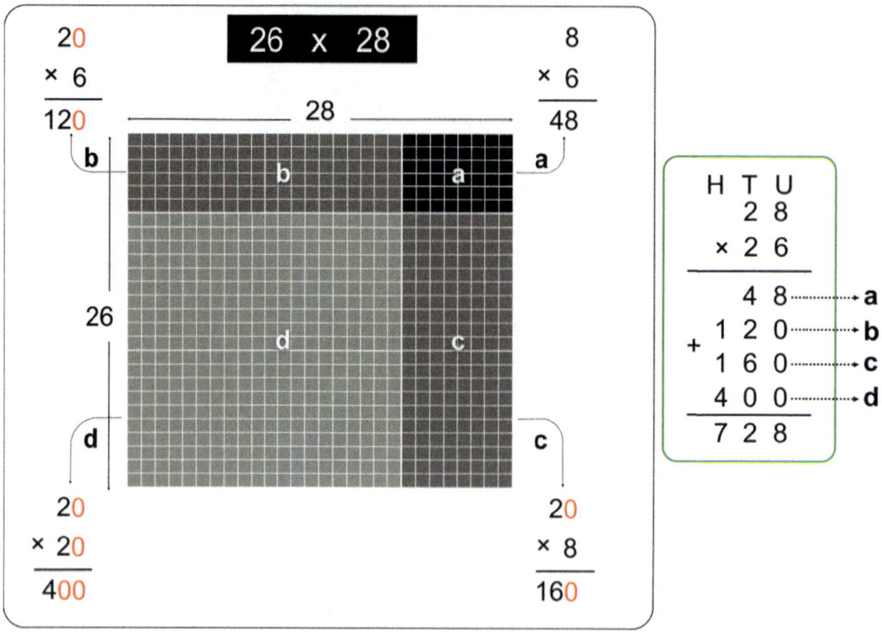

Now try doing this yourself. Begin by drawing a rectangle, then proceeding with the marking of the sides to split the numbers into Tens and Units. These are shown below:

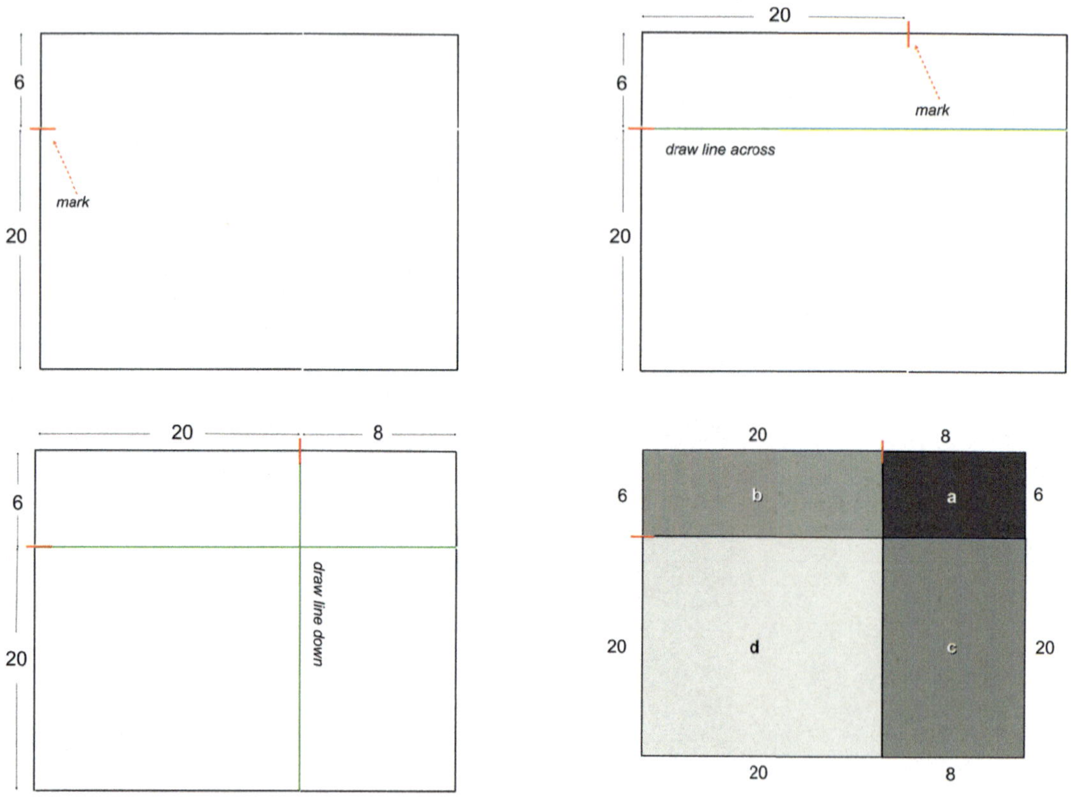

All numbers with multiples of 10 (like 24, 36, 45) will split at 20, 30, 40 and so on.

With enough practice, the following long multiplications may feel easy to do. If you don't know your tables, you may need to consult the ones provided in earlier sections.

The visualisation templates serve as a scaffolding, a form of guided support to enable you to do long multiplication. When you do enough of them, it will get encoded into *your* zone of Mathematical Understanding. Try the following without the visual scaffolding, although the templates for long multiplication have been reproduced for you below:

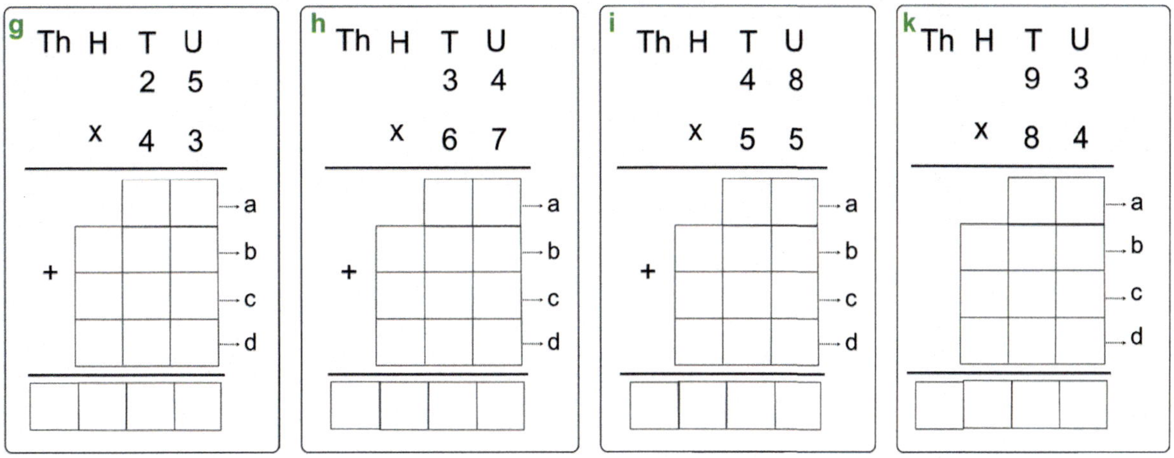

Encoding the Simple Division Operation

A. Using the Operational Symbol for Division

The Operational symbol for Division introduced in Stage 1, is shown below as a simple Dividing Room:

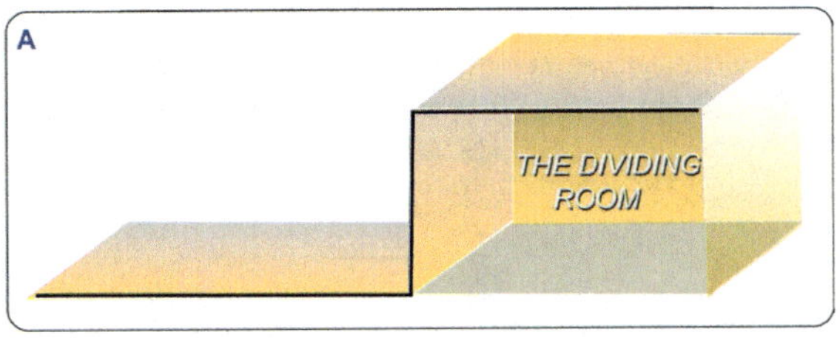

All the things to be divided go inside the room, while those who receive their shares, wait outside the Dividing Room on a broad plank. Below, 10 apples are to be divided between 2 people, or:

10 ÷ 2

The details of the division operation are shown below. Inside the room, 10 apples are broken into 2 equal groups, one for each recipient. They are removed and placed on the roof of the Dividing Room. Each person takes away his/her share of 5 apples. All 10 apples are given away and nothing remains.

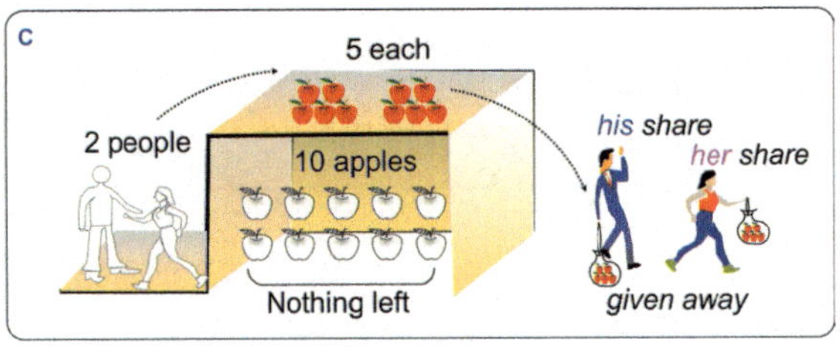

The division operation sign now emerges in a familiar shape and form. They contain 4 basic numbers placed in the order of operation:

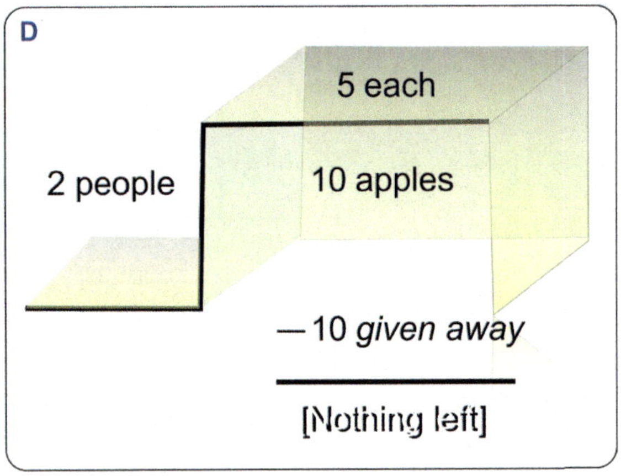

1. 10 apples to be shared are put inside the room.
2. 2 people outside who wait for their shares.
3. 5 items go up on the "roof" to be picked up by each recipient.
4. All 10 apples that have been shared equally, are shown as given away. It is indicated as —10. They are removed from the 10 apples to be shared.
5. Since all 10 apples are gone, there is nothing (zero) left to be shared. This is shown shown below the subtraction line.

This is the protocol that is followed, the most common one, for division. The process of division is shown below, first as an arrangement of arrays (left), then as a division operation using numbers to record the operation numerically (right of Frame **E** below):

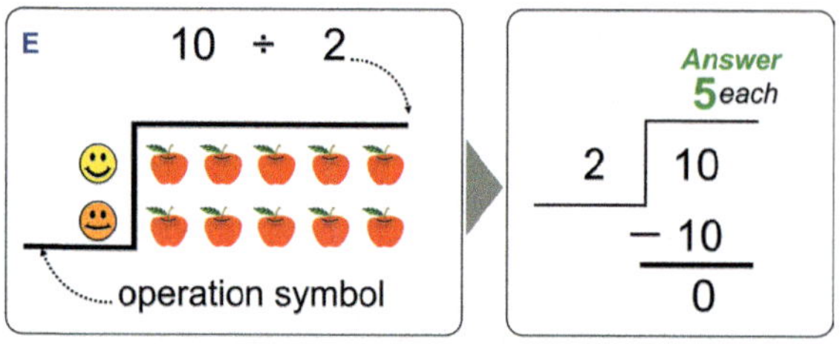

Below (Frame **F**) is another example to show the division 16 ÷ 4. Notice how the numbers are placed to suggest their place values (just as in multiplication, subtraction and addition). This is an example of a 1-step division. The sharing of the entire amount is completed in a single act of removal:

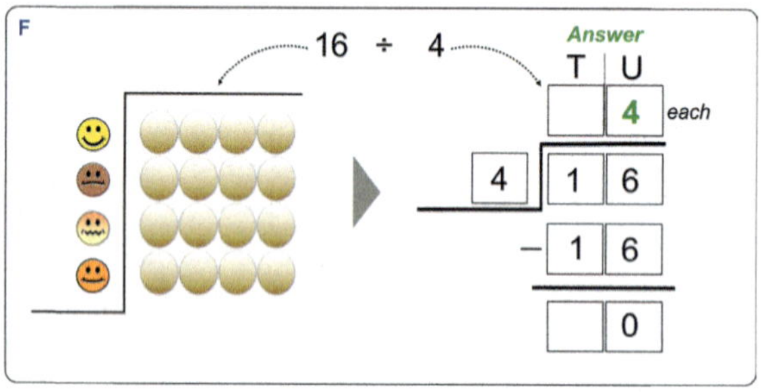

Try the following 1-step division by filling in the empty boxes:

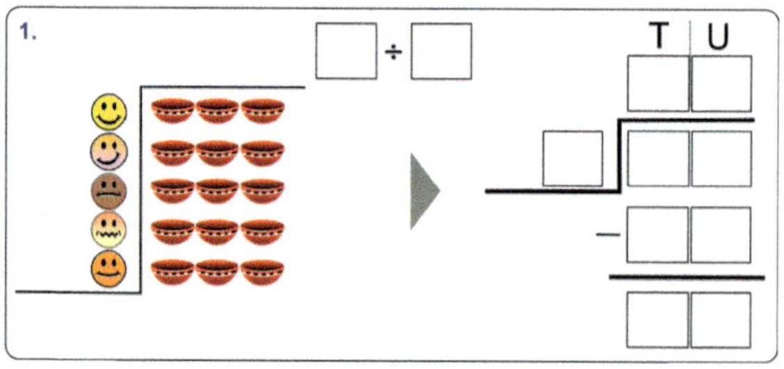

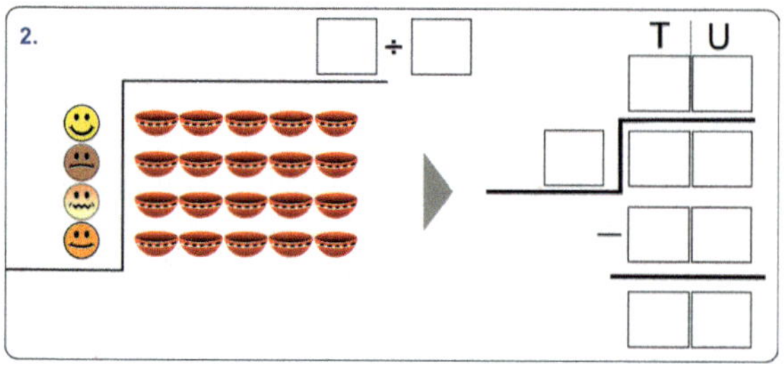

Since the division operation ensures *equal* sharing, unshared amounts remain undivided. For instance when 7 cakes are shared equally between 3 people, only 6 cakes will be given away since each will get 2 cakes.The 1 cake that remains un-shared is shown as a *remainder*. Below, in Frame **3**, 19 soccer balls are shared equally among 3 people. Each gets 6. After they are *given away*, (—18 altogether) 1 soccer ball remains unshared. This is shown visually (left of Frame **3** below) as a division operation, and mirrored numerically (right of Frame **3**). The single soccer ball that dangles below in the left frame is shown as the remainder "1"dangling in the right frame:

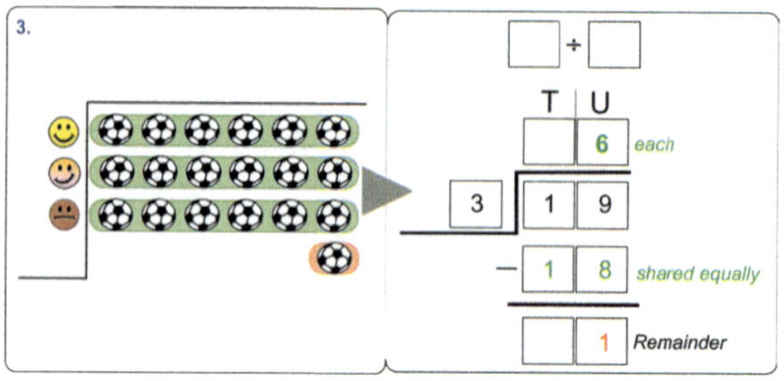

First-time learners draw a visual-numerical correspondence easily, this way. It gets embedded in the long-term memory as something so well understood because the division-operation templates appear perfectly logical.

What numbers will you put in the empty boxes for the division shown in Frames **4** and **5** below?

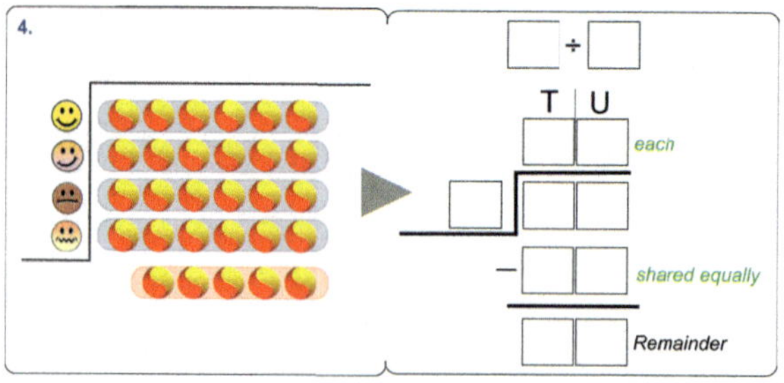

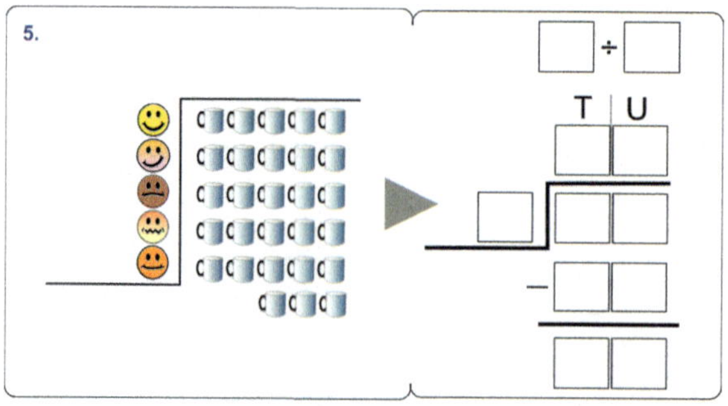

Now take a pencil and paper and try doing the following division sums using the template on the right in Frame **6** below:

6.

a) 19 ÷ 5 b) 23 ÷ 6

x	1	2	3	4	5	6	7	8	9	10	11	12
6	6	12	18	24	30	36	42	48	54	60	66	72

x	1	2	3	4	5	6	7	8	9	10	11	12
7	7	14	21	28	35	42	49	56	63	70	77	84

x	1	2	3	4	5	6	7	8	9	10	11	12
8	8	16	24	32	40	48	56	64	72	80	88	96

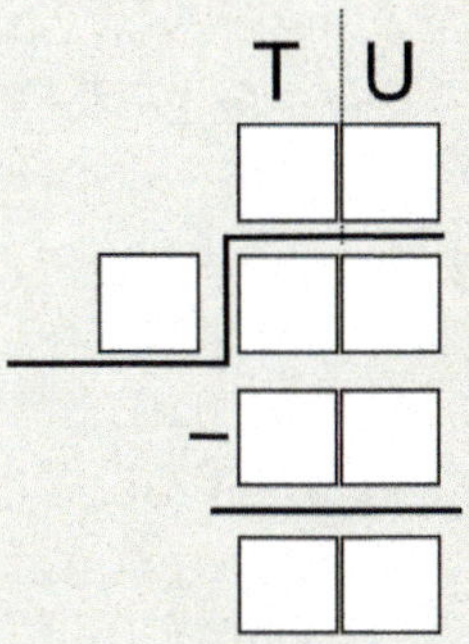

c) 48 ÷ 7 d) 79 ÷ 8

B. Encoding the Long Division Concept

How will you share 4 big slabs and 7 small bars of chocolate equally among 3 people? First share the slabs and bars that *can* be shared equally, right away. That means each gets 1 slab of chocolate and 2 bars (as in Frame **b** below). 1 slab and 1 bar remain unshared

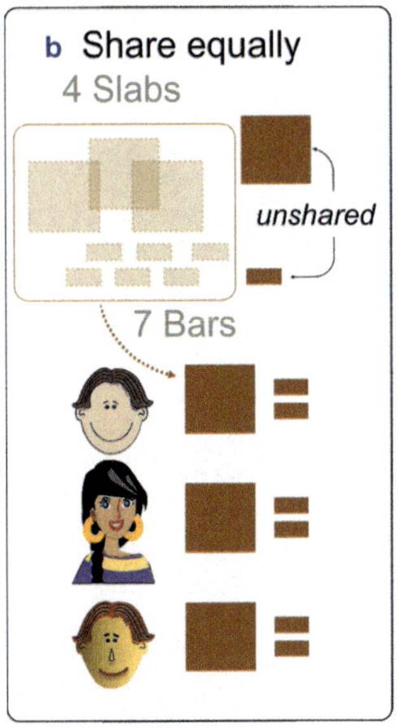

To share 1 *slab* and 1 *bar* equally among the 3 people, we would have to break the slab of chocolate into 3 equal portions (as in Frame **c** above), so each gets one of those portions.

The single remaining bar can be split into 3 smaller but equal portions (as in Frame **d**) and shared:

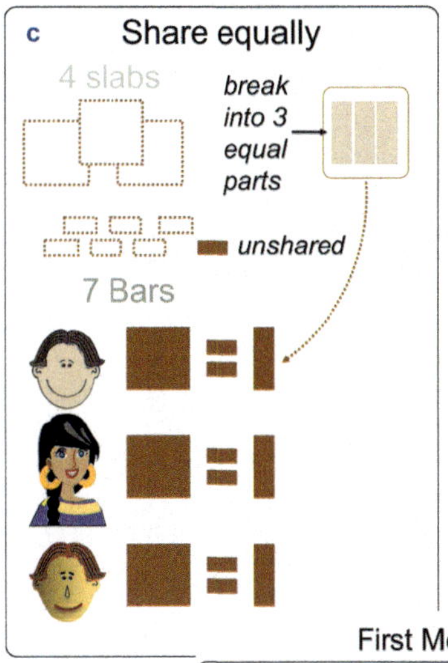

First Method

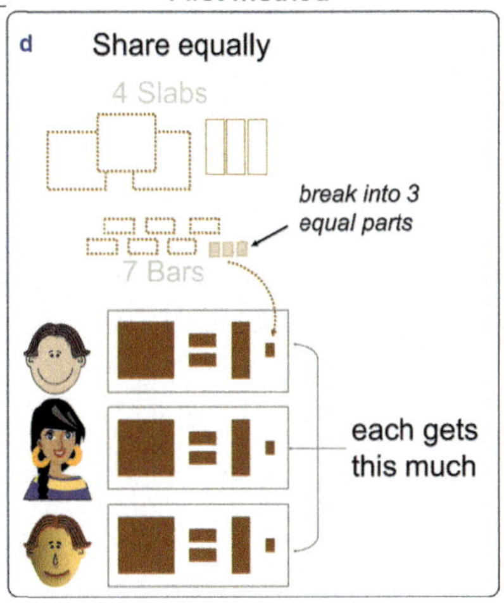

How much chocolate does each get? Answer:1 square slab, 2 small rectangular bars, and a tiny portion of a bar.

If you had to say how much each received you would say: "*1 square slab, 2 small rectangular bars, and a tiny portion of a bar.*"

That sounds pretty awkward. Should equal shares be described as an odd assortment of shapes and numbers in different *unspecified* sizes (how small is small?). Still, this may have been the earliest attempts at long division. Let us call it the **first method.**

A **second**, slightly simpler method would be to cut a slab of chocolate into 8 equal smaller bars. But each of them have to be exactly the same size and shape as the other bars to be shared.

Once again, the problem is posed in **A** below:

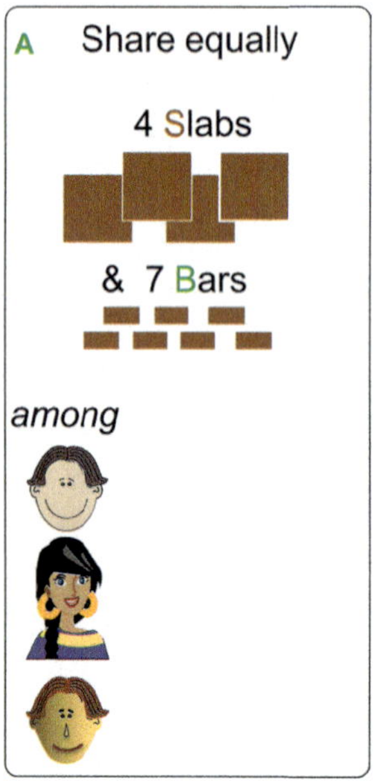

The top section of Frame **B** below shows 3 of the 4 slabs being shared. Each person gets 1 slab. The remaining slab of chocolate is split into 8 equal bars. Their sizes are identical to the 7 bars already there. Now, they all add up to 15 identical bars of chocolate. These are to be shared equally among 3 people:

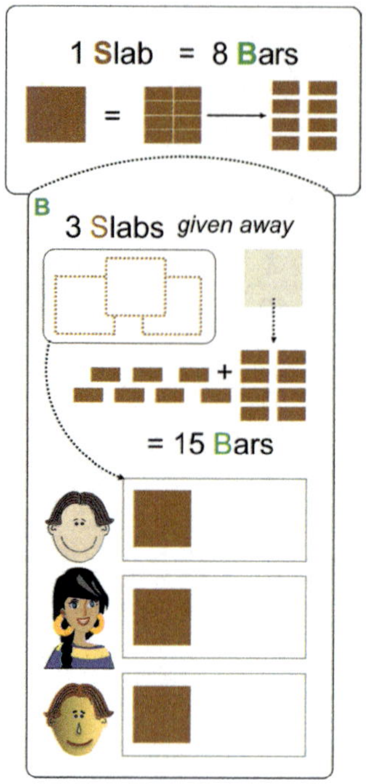

Each person gets 5 bars as shown in **C** below. This time we have a simpler solution. It is easy to put into words. How much did each get? Answer: "*Each received 1 slab and 5 bars of chocolate.*" This is better than the **First Method**.

Whichever method we choose, first or second, both require the breaking up of the larger unit into smaller ones, e.g. slabs into bars. We just have to know how many of the small units (bars) make a big unit (slabs). This makes equal sharing ... or division ... an easy operation to perform.

What if 3 people had to share these amounts equally between themselves: 4 slabs, 6 bars and 2 pieces of chocolate?

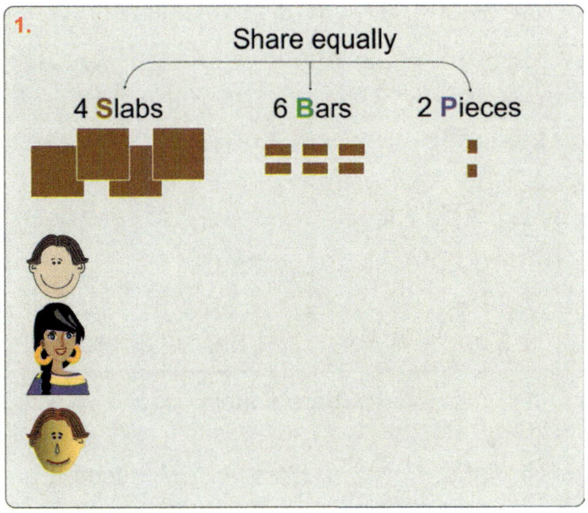

We have created an imaginary world where Units,Tens and Hundreds don't exist. But we can use our visual and numerical reasoning to share equally. It is likely we will bump into all the necessary components of long division. But we will use the Dividing Room and the Slab-to-Bar-to-Pieces conversion shown below:

The long division format will be showing **S B P** (instead of **H T U**):

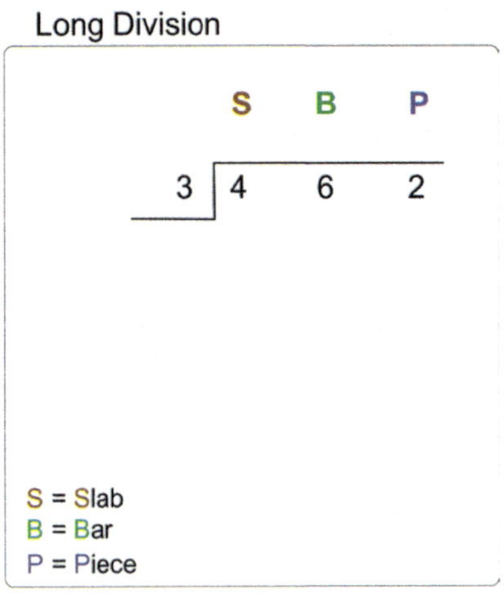

Next we will perform the equal sharing in **Three Steps**:

Step 1: As done earlier, 3 of the 4 slabs will be shared equally among three people. So each gets 1 Slab:

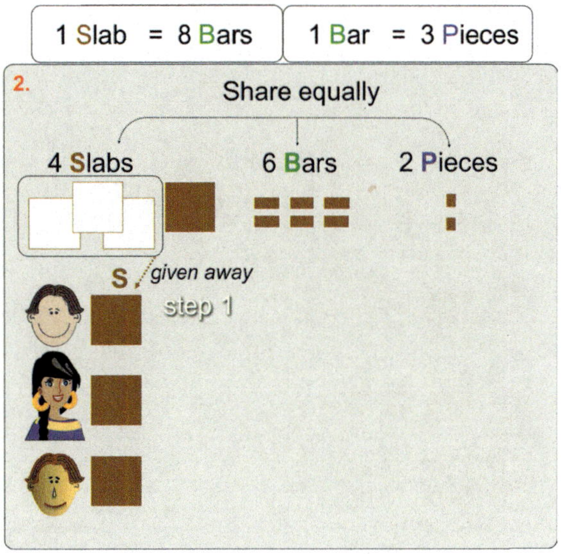

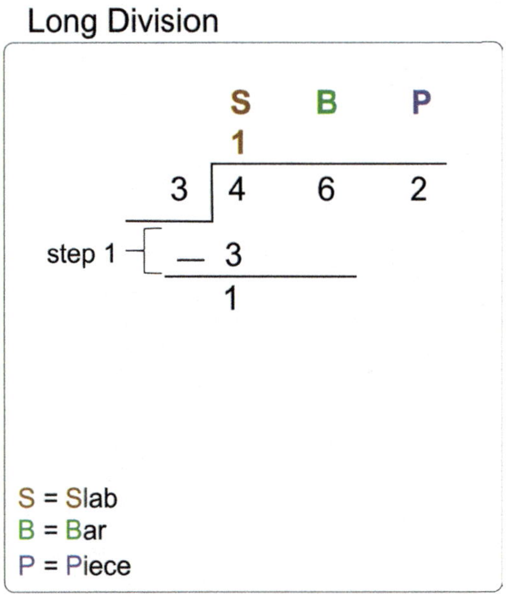

The visual division is shown in the right Frame 2 above, as a numerical operation using the Dividing Room. 1 slab is given to each (**1** is written below **S**), so 3 slabs are removed from 4, with 1 slab left for the next operation.

Step 2: The remaining slab is broken into 8 bars(left of Frame 3 below) then added to the 6 bars that were already there, to make 14 bars. 12 of the 14 bars are equally shared by giving 3 bars to each person. We are now left with 2 bars for the next operation:

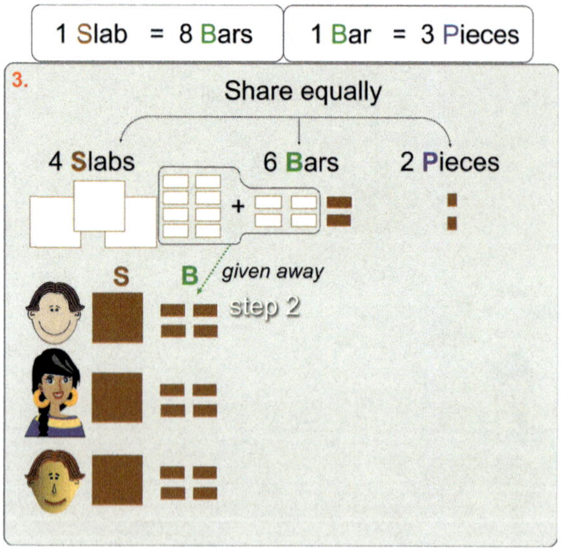

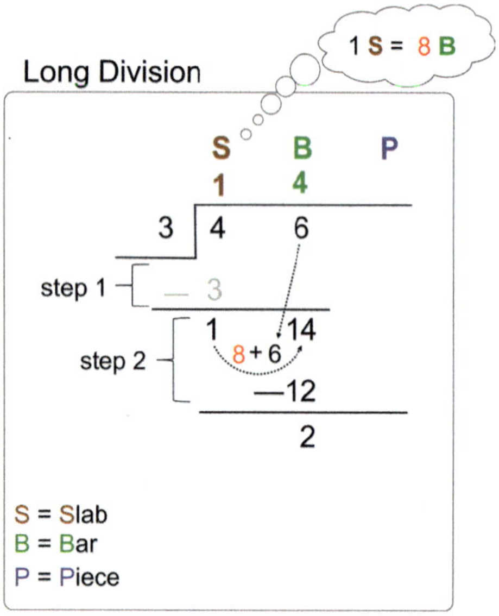

This visual operation is shown numerically in Frame 4 above. First, the 1 remaining slab is converted into 8 bars (the 8 is shown in red) and added to the existing 6 bars, brought down from the top, to become 14 **B**ars (written below **B**). These14 bars are divided among 3 people. Each gets 4 bars. Thus, 12 bars are given away altogether, and 2 bars remain unshared. We move to Step 3.

Step 3: The 2 remaining bars break up into 6 small pieces (since 1 bar = 3 pieces). These join up with the 2 pieces already there, to make 8 pieces altogether. When 8 pieces are divided among 3 people, each gets 2 pieces (left of Frame **4** below). So 6 pieces are given away, still leaving 2 un-shared pieces as remainder:

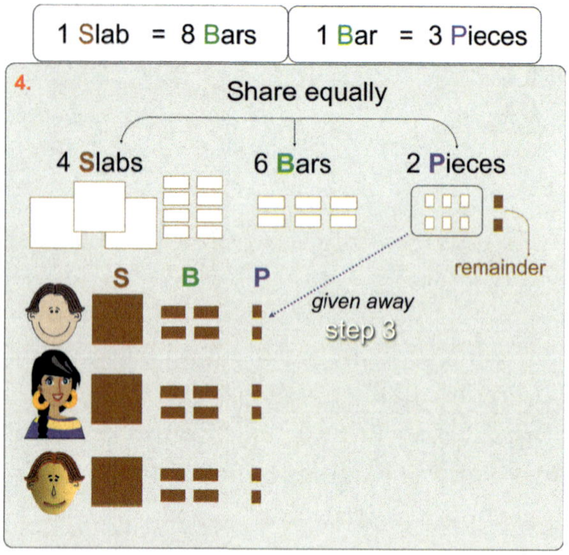

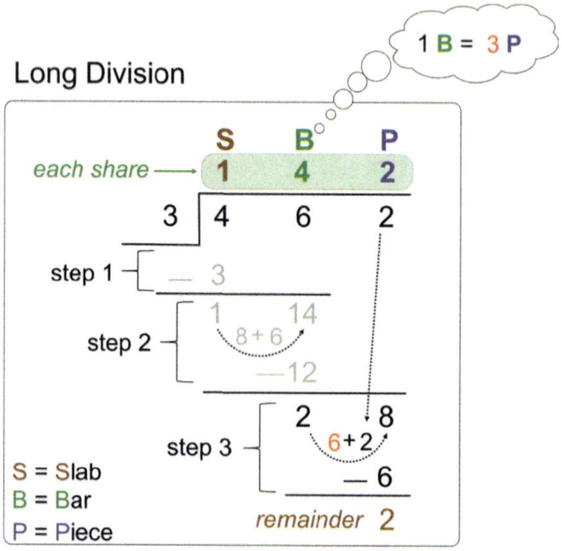

This process is recorded numerically below Frame **4** above. The 2 remaining bars break into 6 pieces (shown in red) and added to the previous 2 pieces that are dropped down. Altogether they make 8 pieces, so 8 is written in the **P**ieces column, below **P**. In Step 3, 8 pieces are divided among 3 people so each gets 2 pieces. Thus, 6 pieces are given away, leaving a final unshared remainder of 2 pieces.

This completes the process of long division, conducted in three steps. The final answer shows the share that each received:

The process is easier to understand if you do not allow your knowledge of Tens, Units and Hundreds to interfere with the reading of the numbers 142 and 462 above. It is not to be read as *"One hundred and forty two"* or *"Four hundred and sixty-two"*. Instead it has to be read as:

"*4 slabs, 6 bars and 2 pieces* of chocolate were divided into three equal shares, each containing *1 slab, 4 bars and 2 pieces of chocolate (with 2 pieces left unshared)*"

Here is an interesting exercise for you to try, knowing that 142 represents Slabs, Bars and Pieces. Make sure you use the conversion below, to get the correct answers:

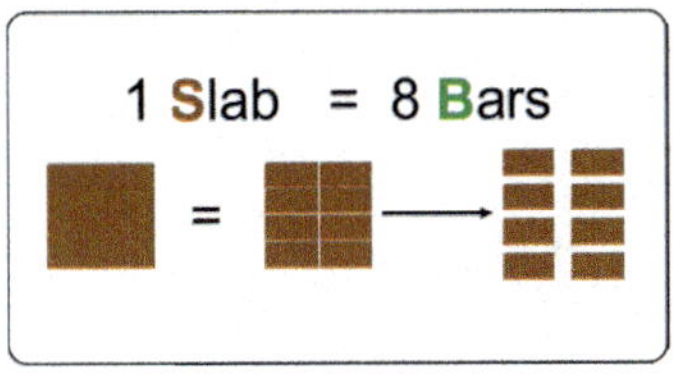

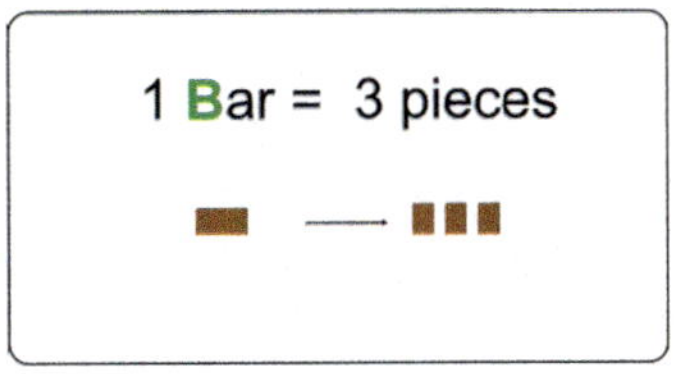

Add these: 142 + 142 + 142

a) *Write the answer in terms of Slabs, Bars and Pieces.*
   (i.e. How many Slabs, Bars and Pieces will they add up to?)
b) *Do they add up to 452? (i.e. 4 Slabs, 5 Bars and 2 Pieces)*
c) *If not, then why not?*

C. Encoding the Long Division Operation

i. 2-Step Long Division

We see a single vein of logic running through long division from beginning to end:

1. The process of division *always* begins with the largest sizes to be divided first, followed by smaller sizes, arranged from left to right. That amounts to breaking larger pieces into smaller pieces.
2. The unshared portions have to be split into smaller sizes for further sharing.
3. At the end, an amount that is less than the number of receivers, is left unshared as the *remainder.*
4. The process ensures the equal sharing of as much of the given quantity as possible, with a very small amount left as a remainder.

We will now show division as a numerical operation alongside the physical act of splitting large slabs into smaller and smaller pieces. This time we will use the HTU Place values because they contain the automatic splitting up of large sizes into smaller sizes. They are also highly standardised, i.e. the bigger size *always* breaks into 10 smaller sizes.

To *divide 43 items among 3 people* is written as: **43 ÷ 3.** This operation is shown below:

x	1	2	3	4	5	6	7	8	9	10	11	12
3	3	6	9	12	15	18	21	24	27	30	33	36

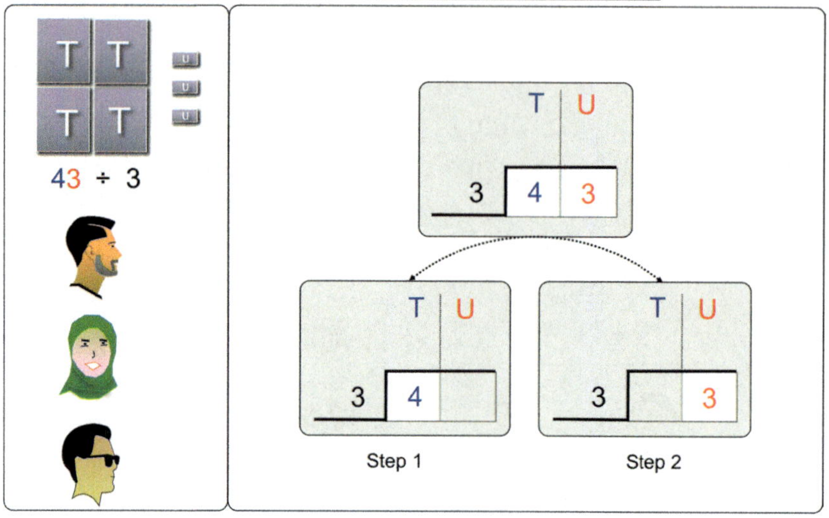

Left Frame (above): 43 is made up 4 Tens (imagine 4 bars of 10) and 3 Units (imagine 3 single pieces).

Right Frame (above): First we will divide the 4 Tens (blue, *Step 1*). Next, we will divide the 3 Units (red, *Step 2*). This is our 2-step plan.

Left frame (below): **Step 1** is shown where 3 of the 4 Tens are divided among 3 people (1 each).

Right frame: **Step 1** is shown numerically as 4 Tens ÷ 3. Each gets **1** Ten and 1 Ten remains un-shared.

x	1	2	3	4	5	6	7	8	9	10	11	12
3	3	6	9	12	15	18	21	24	27	30	33	36

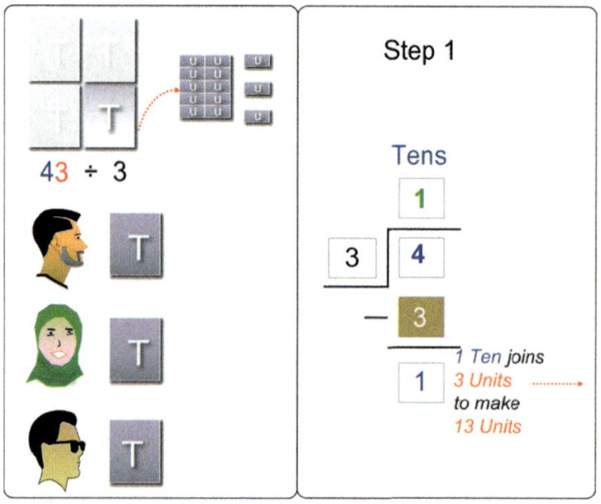

Left frame (below): The 1 unshared Ten is split into 10 smaller Units. These join up with the 3 previous Units to become 13 smaller Units. The 13 Units are divided among 3 people. Each gets 4 Units, and 1 Unit is un-shared (remainder).

Right frame (below): The conversion to 13, followed by division, is shown numerically. First, 3 Units are *dropped* down to join the 10 Units (red arrow) to become 13 Units. When divided the second time, by 3, each gets **4** Units:

x	1	2	3	4	5	6	7	8	9	10	11	12
3	3	6	9	12	15	18	21	24	27	30	33	36

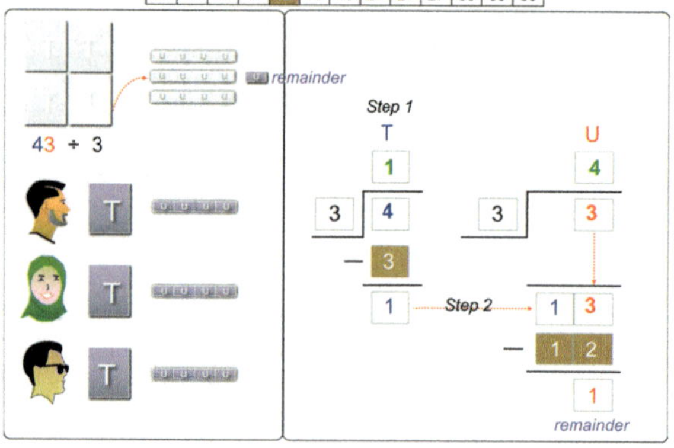

Right frame (below): Step 1 and Step 2 appear as a single continuous 2-step operation right up to the final remainder, 1:

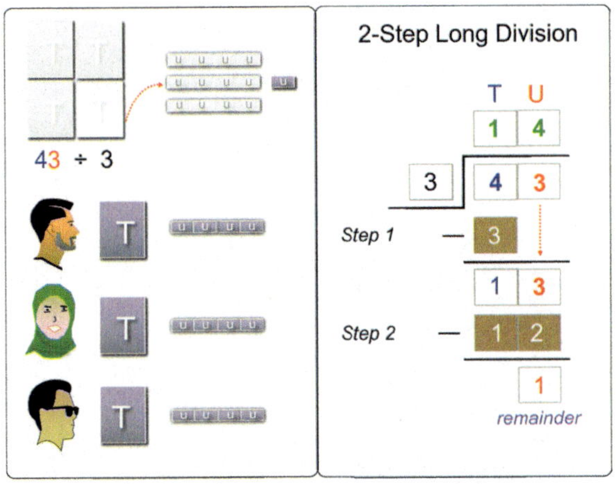

In the end, the 2-step long division gives us the final result: thus, when \$43 is shared equally between 3 people, each will get \$**14** (the answer, in green) and \$**1** will be left, unshared.

Bottom Right Frame: How can we tell if the answer is correct? Is there a way to check it? Sure. All you have to do is multiply the amounts each received (\$14) by 3 (people) to calculate the total amount they shared among themselves. The answer comes to \$42. Add the remaining, unshared \$1 to this and we get back the original \$43.

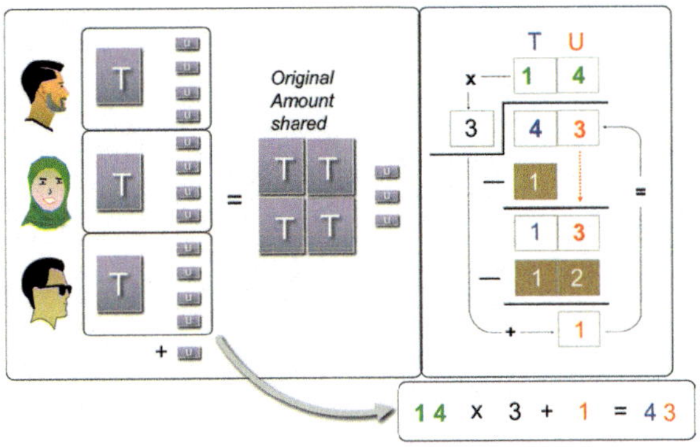

An example of a 2-step long division, **98 ÷ 4**, is shown in the left frame below. Try doing the one given in the right frame, using the same long division template, in 2 steps.

If this is starting to feel easy, try the following 2-step long division:

a) 56 ÷ 3; b) 79 ÷ 4; c) 68 ÷ 5

d) 97 ÷ 6; e) 98 ÷ 8

x	1	2	3	4	5	6	7	8	9	10	11	12
4	4	8	12	16	20	24	28	32	36	40	44	48

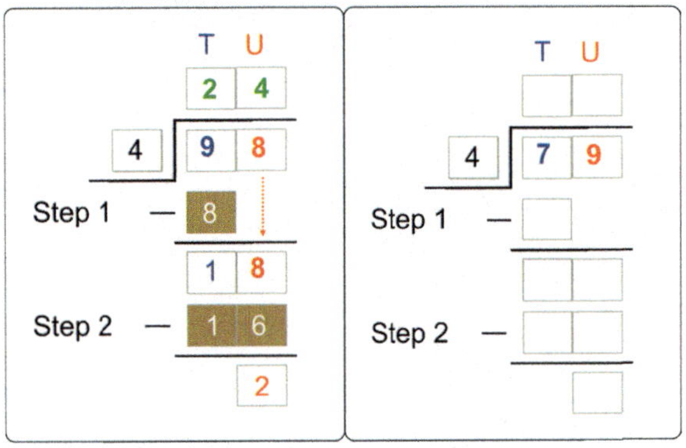

ii. 3-Step Long Division

The larger the number, the more the steps. A 3-digit number will contain three sizes: Hundreds, Tens, and Units, so two conversions and 3 steps. Like this one, which shows 436 items to be shared among 3 people:

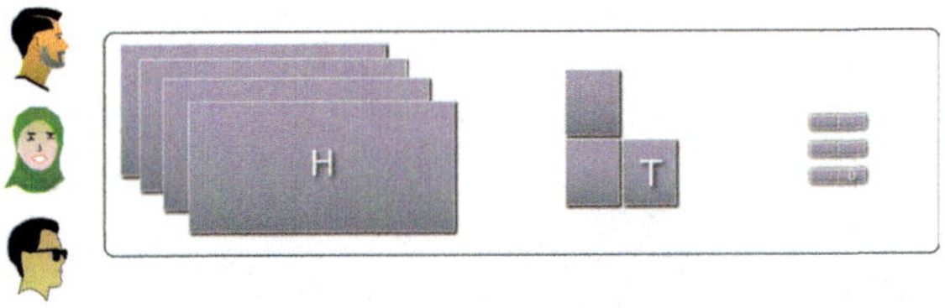

This will be a 3-step long division as planned below. First we divide the Hundreds, next the Tens and finally the Units, each by 3:

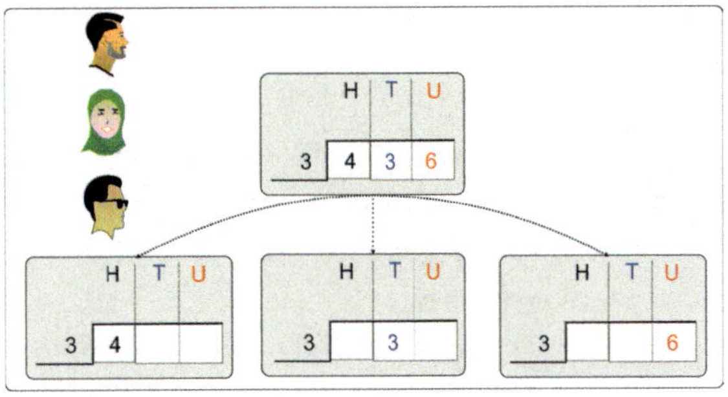

Step 1

Below, Step 1 shows the 4 Hundreds being divided by 3. Each one gets 1 Hundred, leaving one un-shared Hundred:

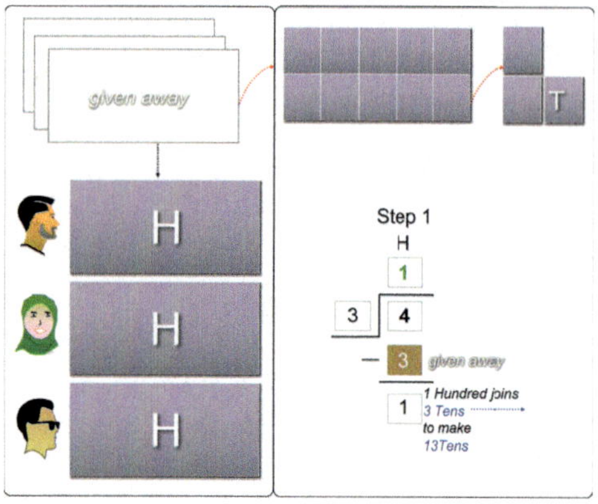

The un-shared 1 Hundred is on its way to get split into 10 Tens, and join up with the previous 3 Tens to become 13 Tens in Step 2(below).

Step 2

Next, the 13 Tens are divided among 3 people:

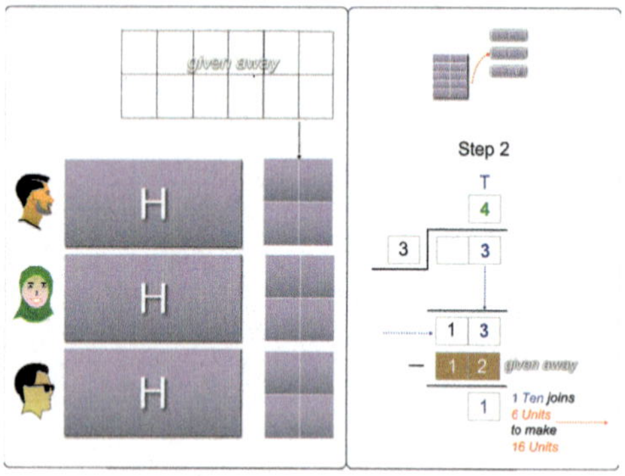

Each receives **4** Tens, and 1 remaining Ten gets split up into 10 Units to join the 3 Units already there.

Step 3 (below) shows the making of 16 Units. These are divided into 3 equal shares. Since 15 can be shared equally among 3, each gets 5 Units, leaving 1 Unit as the final un-shared remainder:

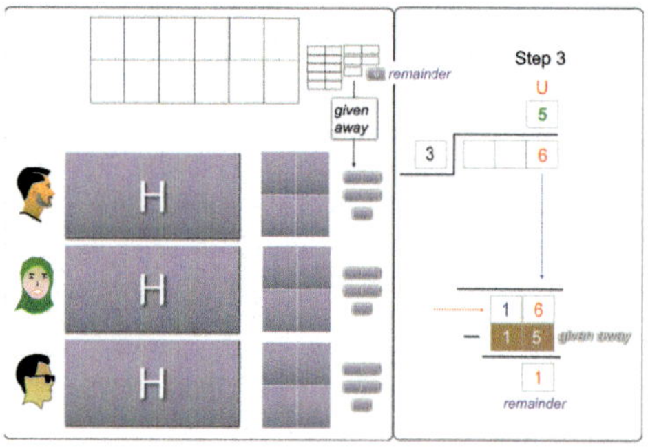

Here is the final answer. Each person gets an amount of 145. 1 Unit is the final reminder:

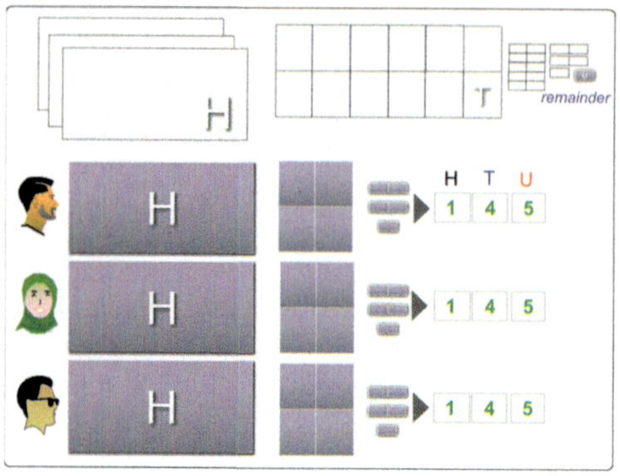

The three Steps are integrated into a single set of three vertical operations. Each step involves the splitting of bigger parts into into smaller parts, followed by the division of those parts. It is a repetitive process and can continue if larger (or longer) numbers are shared equally this way:

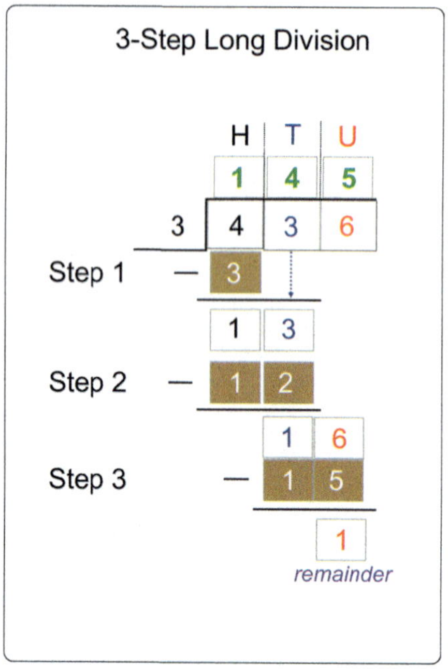

Once again, it is always good practice to verify if the answer is correct. Since each person received \$145, then all three would have shared 3 × \$145 = \$435 among themselves:

Add the \$1 that was not shared and we get \$435 + \$1 = \$436, the original amount.

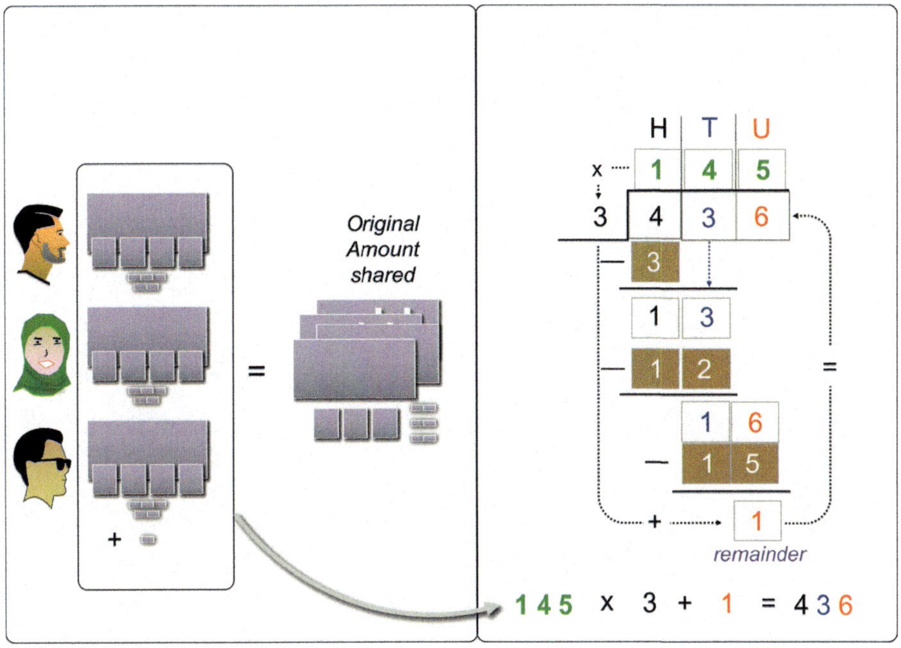

Here is another example of a 3-step long division: **698 ÷ 4**.

x	1	2	3	4	5	6	7	8	9	10	11	12
4	4	8	12	16	20	24	28	32	36	40	44	48

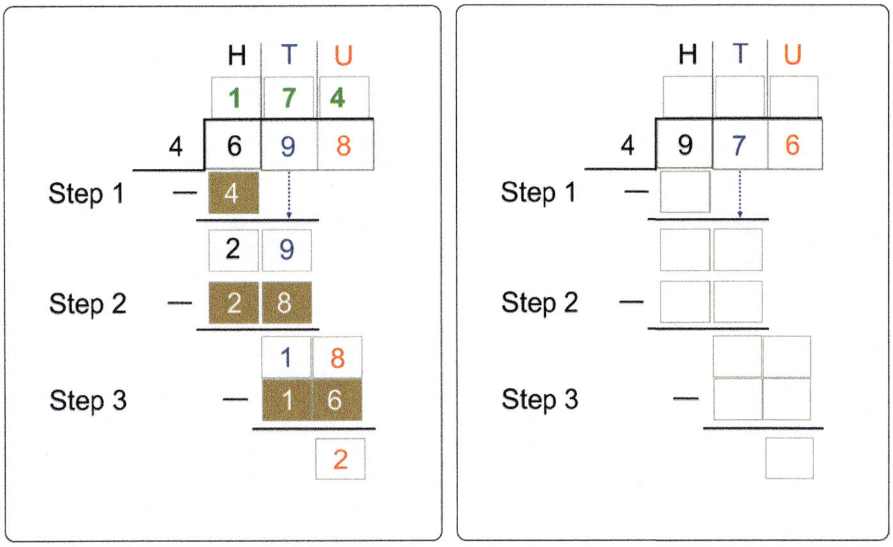

Now try doing the division 976 ÷ 4 given in the right frame above. If you do it easily, proceed with the following on your own, modelling it in the same way:

a) 835 ÷ 5; b) 478 ÷ 4; c) 691 ÷ 6; d) 835 ÷ 7; e) 700 ÷ 8

D. Encoding Division as Equal Grouping

Earlier, in Stage 1, we learned to encode the division symbol in three different ways: left-to-right (for writing a division statement), right-to-left (as a symbol for operation) and top-to-bottom (the "homographic" symbol) which is also used in fractions.

In Stage 1, the Division Concept was understood to mean equal sharing and encoded accordingly. A second concept associated with division denotes equal grouping. It is very distinct and different from the first. For instance, how would you answer this question?

"There are 40 candles that have to be put on small shelves in a church. A shelf can hold 8 candles. How many shelves are needed for all 40 candles?"

It amounts to asking: *"How many groups of 8 candles can be made with 40 candles?"*

The process of "dividing" would mean finding out how many "groups of 8" can be made with 40 candles:

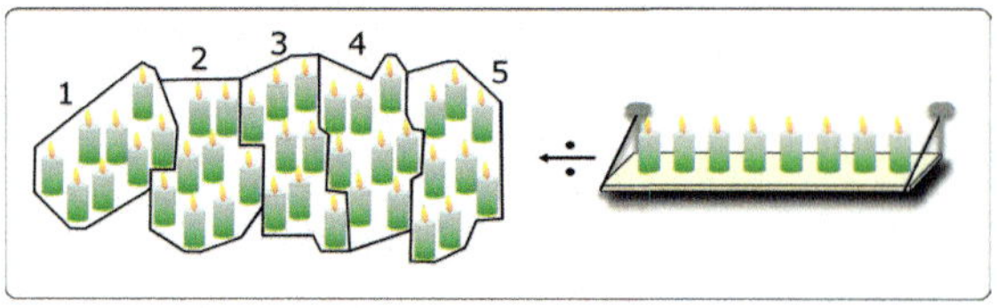

The answer, of course, is "5 groups of 8 candles" and that works out to be 5 shelves:

40 candles ÷ 8 candles = 5 *shelves*

8) 40 = 5 *shelves*

$$\frac{\textbf{40}\text{ candles}}{\textbf{8}\text{ candles}} = \textbf{5 shelves}$$

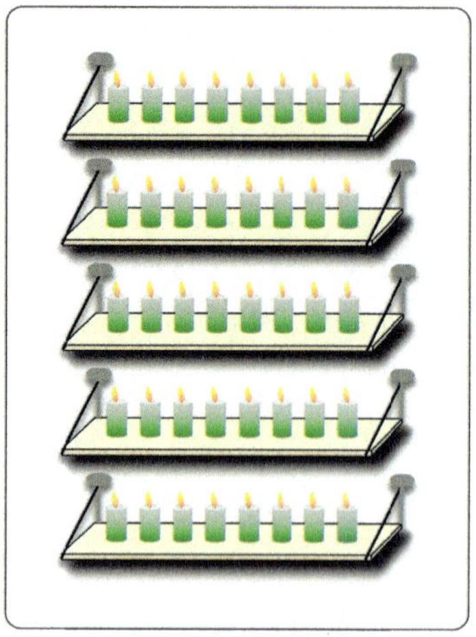

The difference between "division as equal sharing" and "division as equal grouping" is a subtle and confusing one for many who were taught both at the same time, with little or no explanation. Often the confusion is "what" quantity is to be divided by "which" quantity to give "a quantity" of "what"! The difference between the two types of division has to be explained, demonstrated and practised repeatedly until it feels almost intuitive.

This is an excellent example of how we extend the scope of our Deep Knowledge System.

Often the confusion over division arises when distinguishing equal sharing from equal grouping. In equal sharing, there are two *actors:* (i) the number of *things* being shared equally and (ii) the number of *receivers of equal shares.* They are different e.g. apples and people.

In equal grouping, the two actors happen to be the same: both are apples. Furthermore, a new, *passive receiver* is introduced: a pack, a crate, a box, basket, or any container that contains the answer.

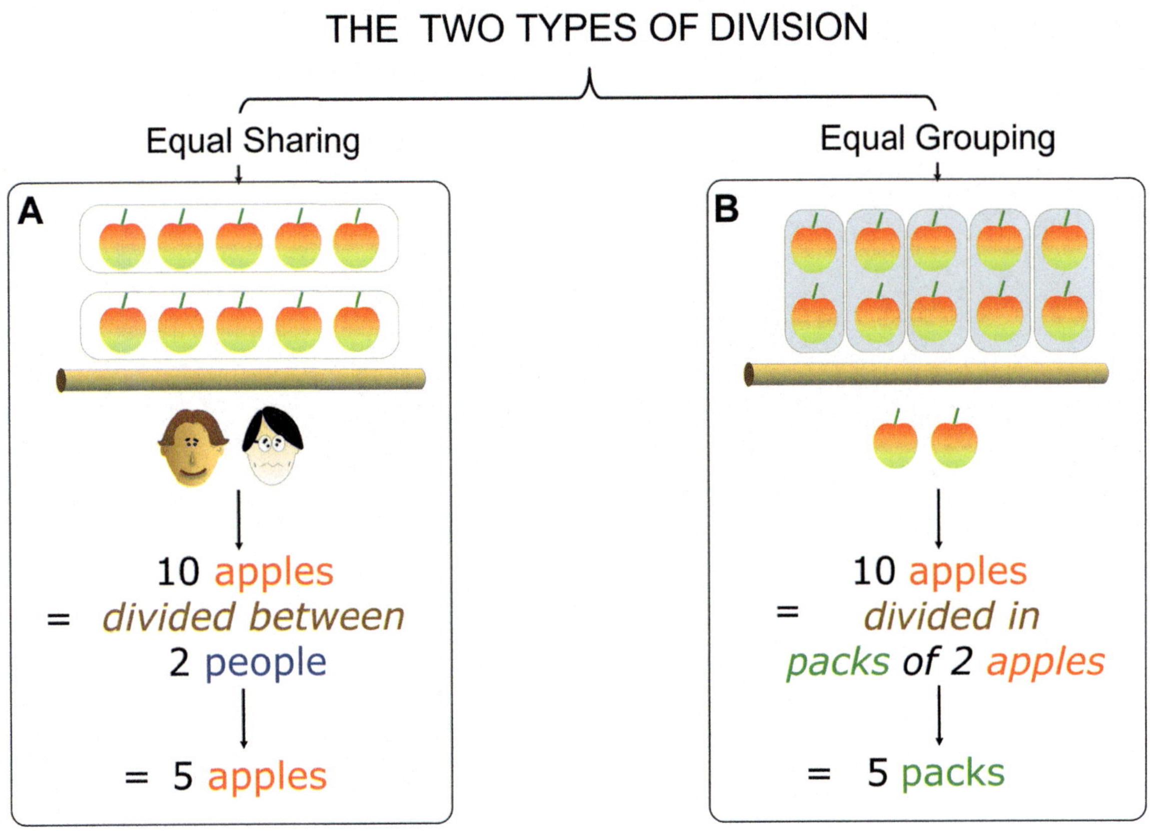
THE TWO TYPES OF DIVISION
Equal Sharing
Equal Grouping
A
10 apples
= divided between
2 people
= 5 apples
B
10 apples
= divided in
packs of 2 apples
= 5 packs

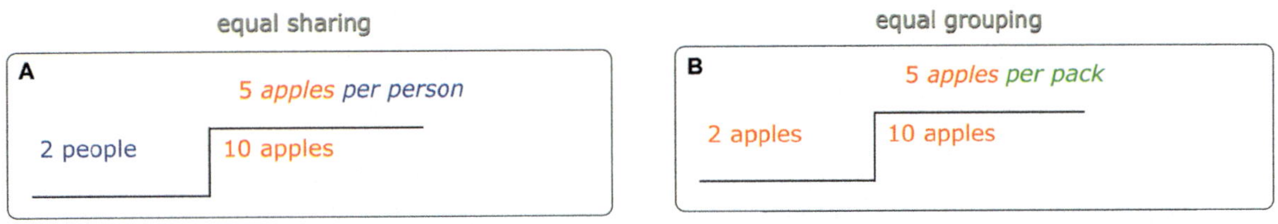
equal sharing
A
5 apples per person
2 people
10 apples
equal grouping
B
5 apples per pack
2 apples
10 apples

Encoding Properties and Behaviours of Circles

It is easy to obtain a conceptual understanding of "roundness" because it is associated with the behaviour of the ball and the wheel (roll, bounce):

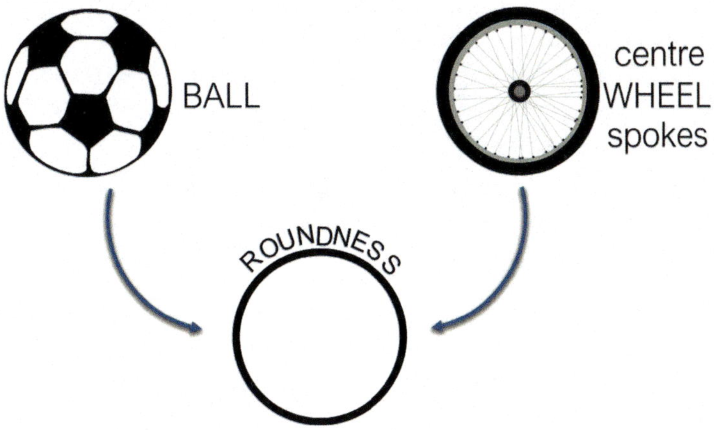

The wheel is a great source for exploration because we feel its "mathematicality" long before it is taught in schools. It is embossed in our DKS. For example, how can we tell how big a wheel is? How do we indicate its size? Our Deep Knowledge System will intuitively do it this way:

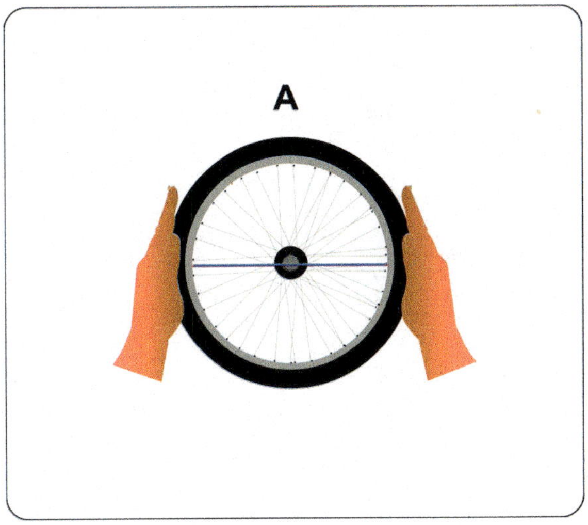

Leaving out the wheel's rubber, the blue line in frame A represents the size of the metallic inner wheel quite correctly. Some might even discern that the blue line is composed of a pair of spokes joined at the centre, along a straight line.

It can also be shown this way:

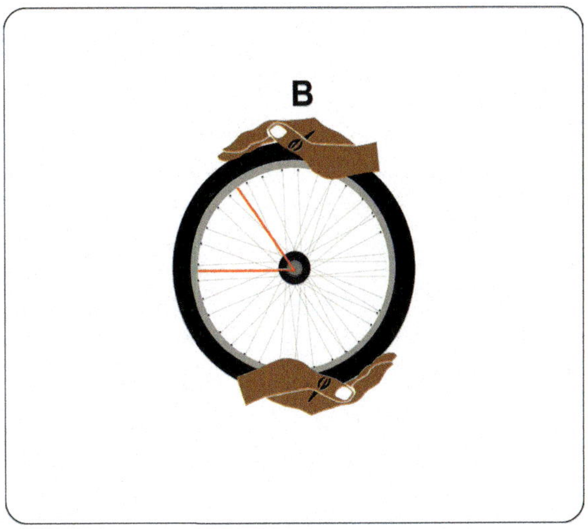

However counter-intuitive it may appear the first time, our DKS will accept that the two red spokes, being the same size, will always add up, to give the **Wheel Size** shown by the blue line. And, no matter what the size of the wheel, this relationship between wheel size and spokes will remain unchanged:

How Big is the Wheel?

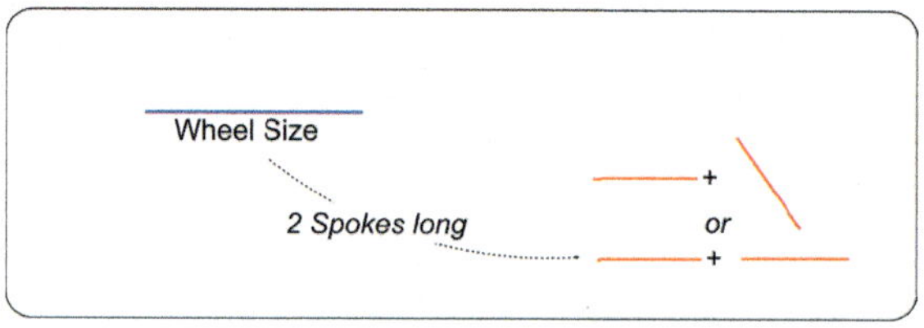

This "rule" can be drawn from simple exploratory investigations in the classroom or at home. It can be encoded just to be understood the mathematical way:

Encode this:

Wheel size = W Spoke = S

Wheel size = 2 Spokes

W = 2 S

(for all wheels)

"For all wheels" signifies a great leap in human thinking, for it suggests "for all circle sizes". The act of encoding of mathematical "truths" anticipates algorithmic thinking which is introduced in Stage 5. However, that stage does not suddenly descend from above upon the completion of Stage 4. It is a slow, steady climb all the way, and the journey begins from Stage 2.

Encoding conceptual understanding is like sealing and protecting understood concepts with a fine mebrane. It reguates whatever enters the core concepts by filtering out extraneous elements. In a sense, pre-encoded conceptual understanding is very vulnerable. Learners often confuse a target concept with another, or link it up to its offshoots, and this usually results in muddled thinking. This is less likely to happen if a concept, once fully understood, is fenced in by being encoded. So: W = 2S.

All children have a rational-intuitive knowledge of wheels of varying sizes. They have some idea that small or large wheels cover different distances in a single turn:

Which one will roll further?

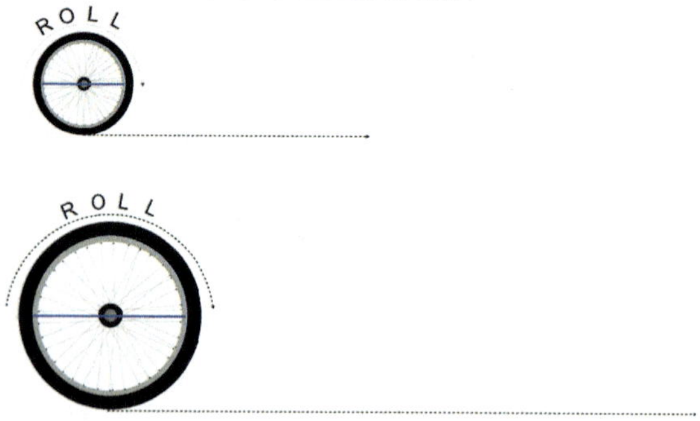

It will not take very long for young learners to realise that in a single turn, the smaller wheel will cover a shorter distance. So an investigation can begin with the simple question: "How far does a wheel move in one single turn?"

Shown below is a wheel with an orange arrow at the bottom to indicate its start position. The pair of joined spokes are shown in blue, and the single spoke, in red. Suppose the single spoke is 4 cm long. That means the blue double-spoke is 8 cm long:

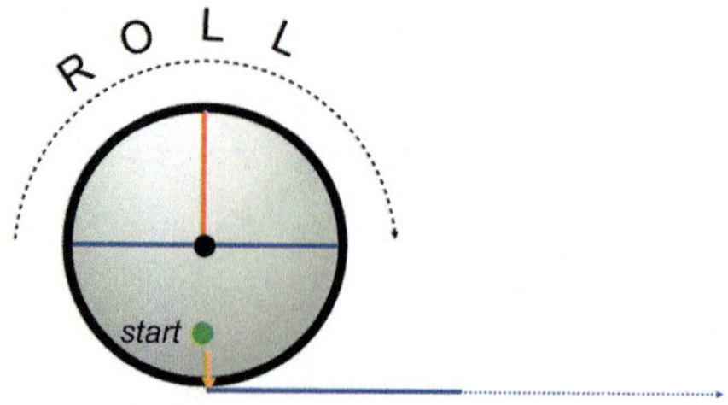

As shown below, the first half-turn is completed when the orange arrow reaches the top of the circle (center) and the red spoke moves to the bottom:

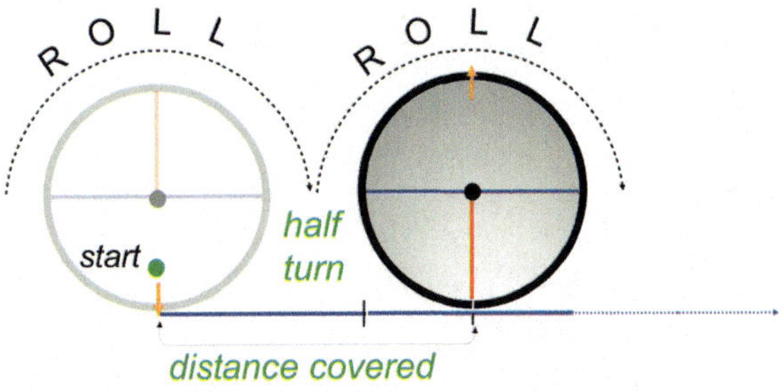

What do you notice about the distance it moved during the first half-turn? We can mark that distance by drawing a line (in blue) from the start position to the point vertically below the second orange indicator. If measured in cms, it should be around 12 cm. Or 1½ × wheel size.

Below we see the wheel completing the second-half turn. The orange arrow has returned to its original position and so has the red spoke:

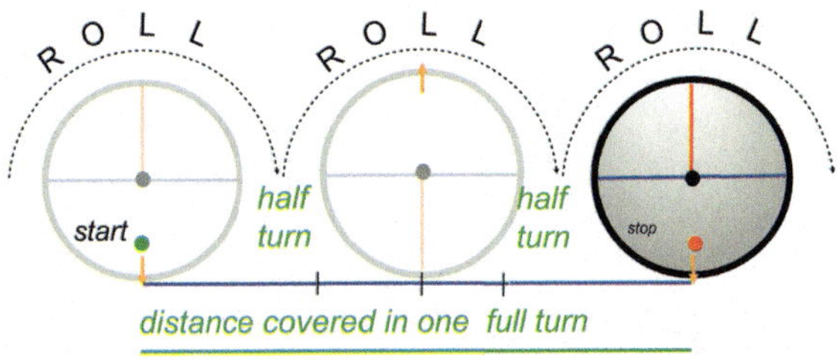

The distance the wheel moved during a single full turn is shown as the green line. It is equal to the length of the blue line which has covered yet another 1½ × wheel size. Altogether that makes:

1 ½ +1 ½= 3 Wheel sizes.

If we measure it, the distance will be around 24 cm (slightly more than 24 cm).

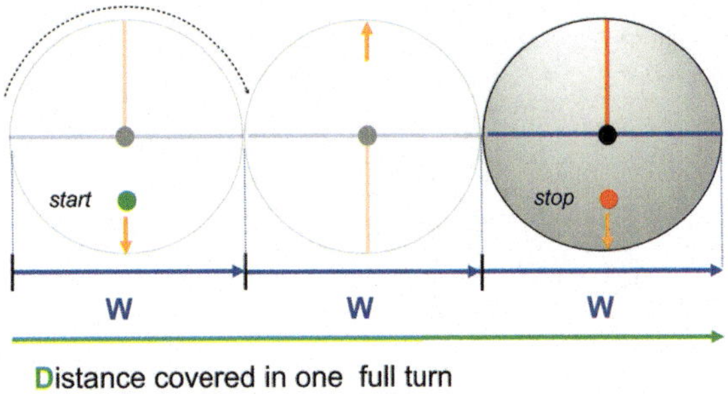

We encode all that has been understood, in this way:

Encode this:

Distance Covered in 1Turn = **D** **W**heel size = **W**

Distance Covered in 1Turn = 3 **W**heel Sizes

D = 3 **W**

(for all wheels)

With enough practice learners will be able to decode this at a glance, to mean:

> *"Take any wheel size. If you want to know what distance it will move in one turn, then imagine three of them joined rim to rim. The total length of 3 joined wheel sizes is the length it will move in 1 complete turn."*

So if the wheel size is 10 cm. Then the wheel will move 3 × 10 cm = 30 cm, in a single turn.

The more learners practice encoding their conceptual understanding of mathematics, the easier they will be able to recall it. "How far will a wheel of size 25 cm go in if it turns 3 times?" Most readers will be able to work such problems out with ease:

If it turns once, the distance moved will equal the length of 3 wheel sizes

When it turns 3 times that will be: 3 times (*3 wheel sizes*) = *9 wheel sizes.*

So if each wheel size is 25 cm, then 9 wheel-sizes will be 9 × 25 cm = 225 cm

Here are two problems that might pique the interest of those who like to be challenged:

1. If a wheel covers a distance of 150 cm in a single turn, what is the size of the wheel?
2. After turning 10 times, a wheel covers a distance of 450 cm. What is the size of the wheel?

Our Deep Knowledge System remains connected throughout. We are taking it all in, as we would any common-sensical, logical statement. As a result, we can reach into problems from inside, and work our way outwards to decode the encoded and solve problems.

As learners get increasingly exposed to the process of encoding their conceptual understanding, their DKS becomes more elastic. They are able to stretch and access more formal and abstract domains of the Natural Number System. Their comfort zone extends to enter mathematical spaces that once felt very forbidding.

Here is the distance (shown in green) that the wheel had covered in a single turn:

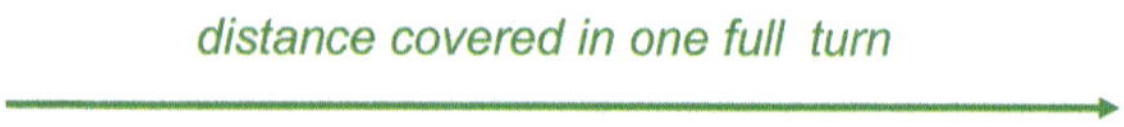

This distance, shown by a length of green ribbon, would wrap right around the wheel completely and fit it perfectly:

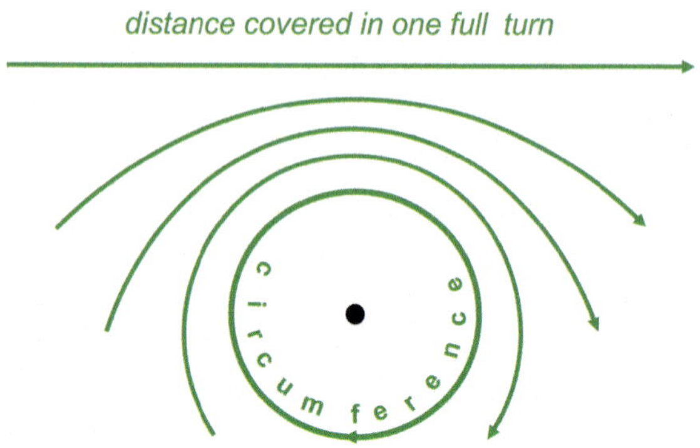

The length of a string that wraps around the wheel to fit it completely will be the same as the distance it moves in a single turn. Only this time we will replace the words "**distance covered in 1 turn**" with its mathematical name:

CIRCUMFERENCE

So: "a wheel covers a distance of 20 cm in 1 turn" can now be stated as: " A wheel has a circumference of 20 cm." Imagine an ant that sits atop a wheel and starts crawling all the way down and around to get back to the top again. To return to the same spot where it started, it covers a distance of 20 cm. That distance covered in one turn is called "**circumference**."

Let us now conceptualise wheels as circles to complete the coded vocabulary used in mathematics:

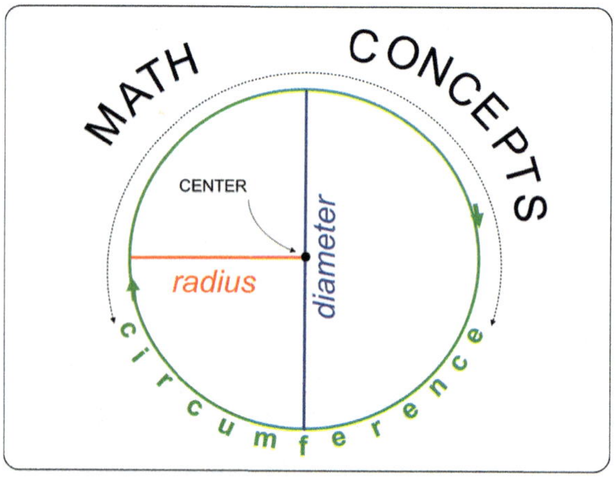

Encode this	in Mathematical Terms
Wheel size = W	Diameter = D
Spoke = S	Radius = R
Wheel size = 2 Spokes	Diameter = 2 Radius
W = 2 S	D = 2 R
(for all wheels)	*(for all circles)*

Encode this	in Mathematical Terms
Distance Covered in 1Turn = D	Circumference = C
Wheel size = W	Diameter = D
Distance Covered in 1Turn = 3 Wheel Sizes	Circumference = 3 x Diameter
D = 3 W	C = 3 D
(for all wheels)	*(for all circles)*

The **S**poke is called the "**Radius**"
The **W**heel-size is called the "**D**iameter"
The **D**istance it moves in 1 turn is called "**C**ircumference (or the length of the circle's boundary).

The new mathematical encoding to replace the earlier ones is shown below:

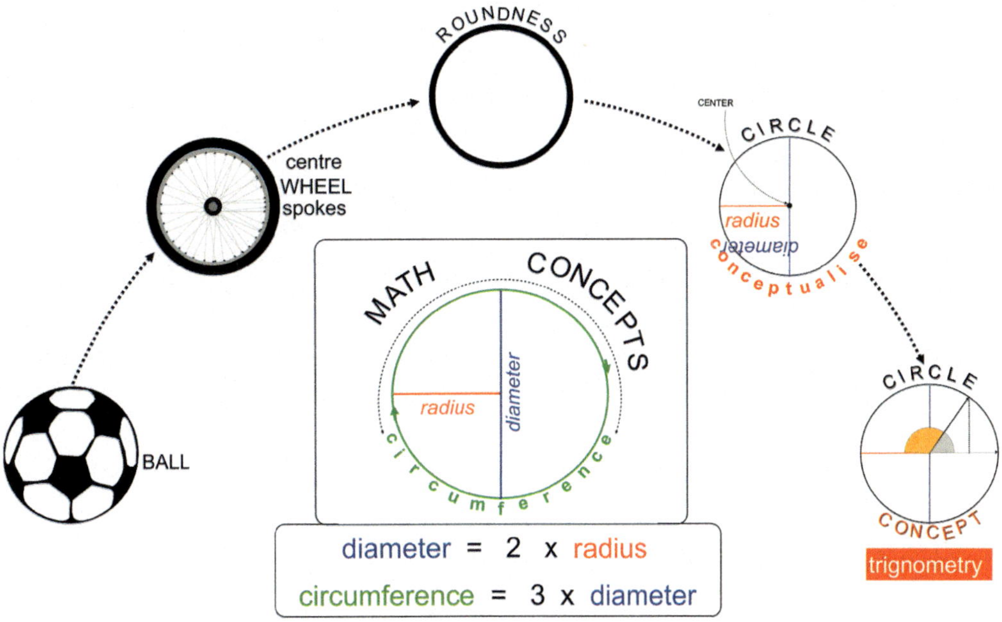

[**Note**: it is not exactly **3 × D**, but a tiny, tiny bit more than **3** times. So the number **3** is a very close approximation]

Another way of demonstrating this is to make a circle with a length of wire. Cut the wire and open it until it becomes a straight line. The length of the line will always be 3 times the length of its diameter:

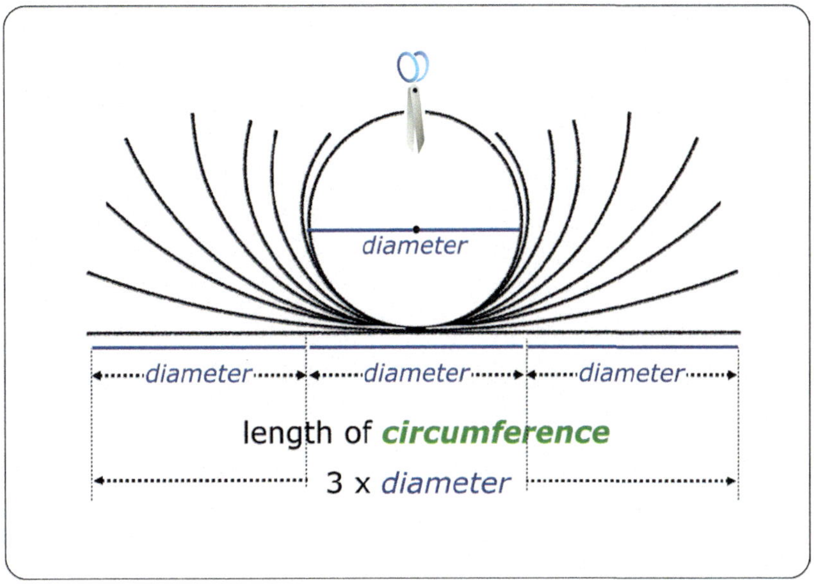

SYMBOLISM 4

Encoding Fractions

A. As Part of a Group of Multiple Units – A

Let us encode fractions as *part of a group of (same) objects*, like a group 9 stars. 9 stars are shown below from which 5 were taken. The 5 stars represent a portion of the taken. The 5 stars represent a portion of the 9 stars, or a *part*. Since each star is a *ninth* of 9 stars, 5 stars will be denoted as "five *ninths*". We can also say: *"5 out of 9"* stars. The line that separates 5 (above) and 9 (below) represents the words *"out of"*:

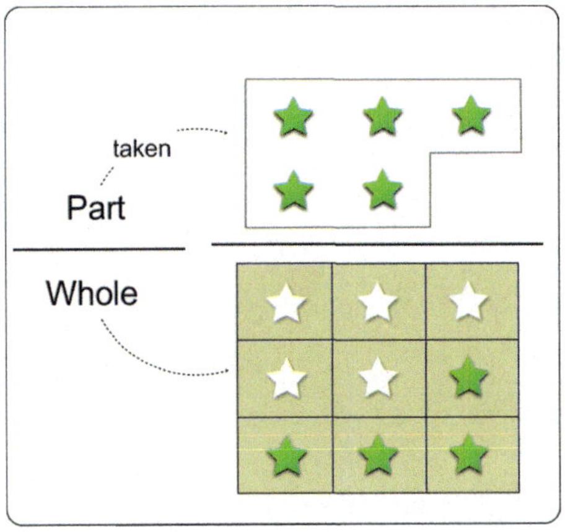

Lower Frame (below): Here is another view. The whole (a batch of 9 stars) is viewed as a single group. Each star is shown as a ***single part***, identical to all the others. So 9 of them behave like " 9 equal parts" within a larger ***single group*** of identical units:

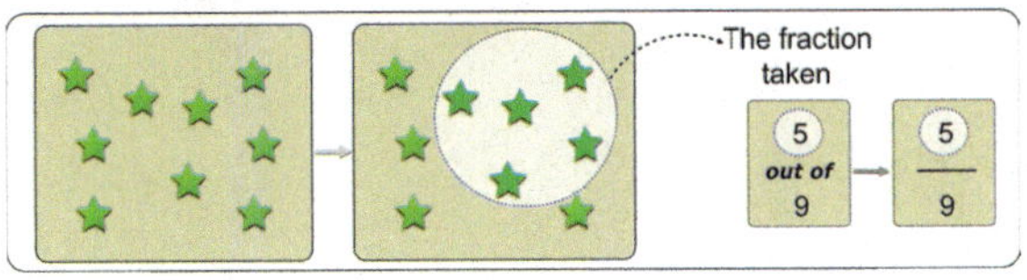

In either case, the fraction taken is decoded as "five *ninths*":

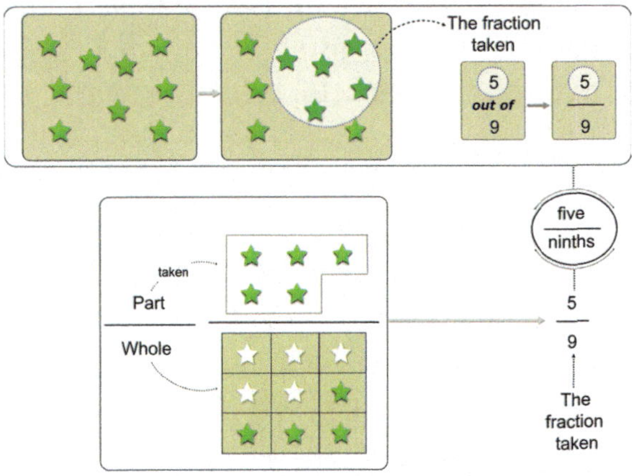

How would you answer the following:

"A shelf contains 18 books, out of which 7 books are hard-bound. The rest are paperbacks:

a) What fraction of the books are hard-bound?
b) What fraction are paperbacks?

You can think in terms of how many out of how many? or what part of what whole? Either way, the answer remains unchanged. It will look like one of these three frames, 1, 2 or 3:

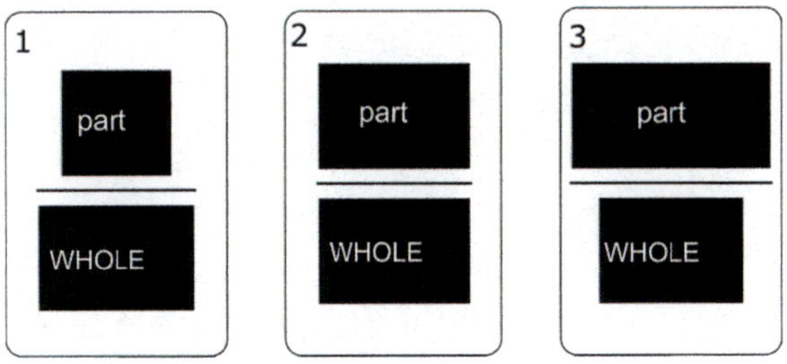

The answer to Q a) will look like Frame 1: hard-bound books will be *7- eighteenths of all the books* with 7 written above 18.

The answer to Q b) will also look like Frame 1: the paperbacks will be *11-eighteenths of all the books with 11 written above 18.*

The answer should be stated orally as a formal fraction, not as "7 out of 18", not "7 over 18" but "7-eighteenths." Why? Because 7 out of 18 can be confused with subtraction and the person listening will conclude: "Oh! So that means 11 books are left!" In fact many will wonder why the fuss? Why are 11 books called "11 out of 18" and not just plain "11 books"!? Why indeed? The reason is: we are expressing the 7 books taken as being a *part of the total number* of books on the shelf. We are not saying how many books were taken. We are saying what portion or part of all the books were taken.

Often, in real life, people are interested not in numbers but in quantitative relationships that tells them what they really want to know and judge. Imagine a concert hall that has 650 seats. If you want to judge the attendance at a concert, you will likely want to know it in terms of few, some, many, almost-full or half-empty. Was it half-full? A quarter? A third? Three-Quarter?...and so on. Not in exact numbers like: 448 out of 650. If you were told that a third of the seats were empty, you can imagine splitting a rectangular array of all seats into three equal parts, and 2 of those parts are full. You need information about a part of the whole. It is just easier to understand and communicate.

Before proceeding to the next encoding section **B**, first-time learners should achieve mastery in encoding fractions up to this point. This means, they should score high on three criteria, when encoding fractions:

1. ***Display accuracy***: they should get all 10 out of 10 fraction encodings right, at their first attempt.
2. ***Display speed***: when accuracy has been achieved, then their speed in encoding should increase to optimal levels.
3. ***Display fluency***: they should be able to do both of the above with ease, and confidence.

B. As Part of a Group of Multiple Units – B

Here is an incomplete request: "Please give me half!" Your Deep Knowledge System, as wide awake as ever, will ask: "Half of what?" Something is missing here, obviously.

When engaging with many single items, like 6 apples, 15 eggs, £30, Rs.50 or $80 each set of items is treated as one large basket containing many single units.

In Step 1 below, we show *half of 6 apples*, in this way:

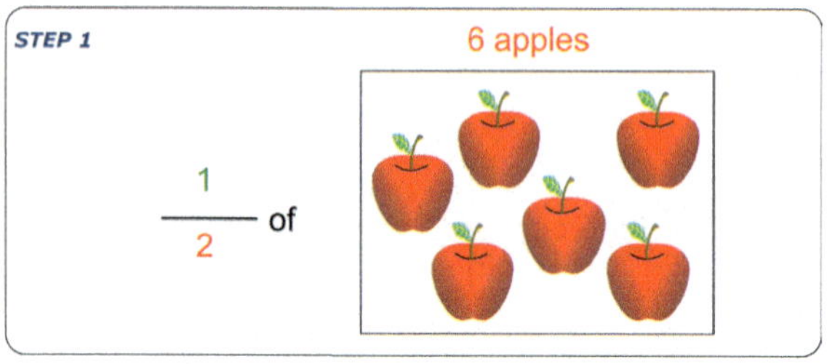

In Step 2, below, we decode the number 2 i.e. show the 6 apples broken into two equal groups of 3:

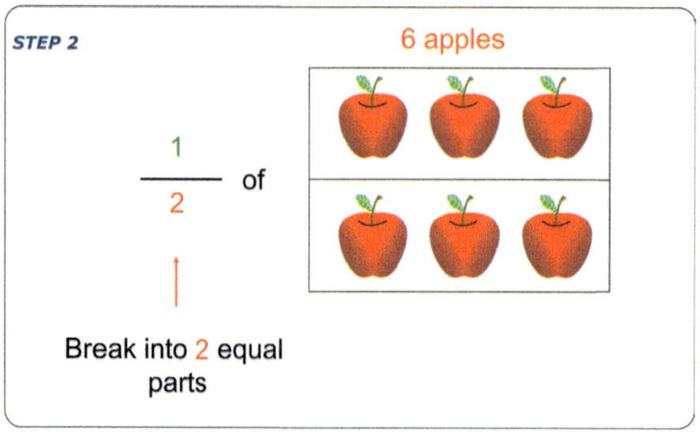

In Step 3, we decode the meaning of the number 1 above the fraction line by Taking 1 of the 2 groups (shaded green), which equals 3 apples:

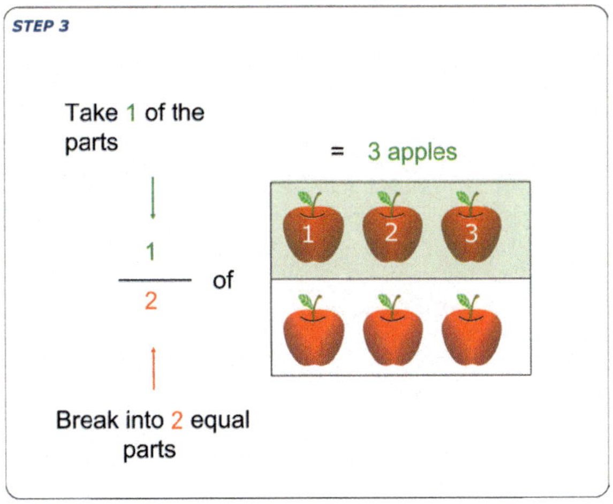

This is the mathematical representation of:

Half of 6 apples = 3 apples

This concept is the gateway to a variety of complex and interesting insights into how to think mathematically. First try finding "three fourths (or 3-quarters) of 8 bananas". Simply decode the meaning of the fraction "three-fourths." What does **4** mean here? What does **3** mean here?

Step 1: first state your intention as a mathematical sentence encoded visually, like this:

Step 2: Decode the meaning of number 4, below the line. It is an encoded instruction: break the bananas in 4 equal groups, as shown:

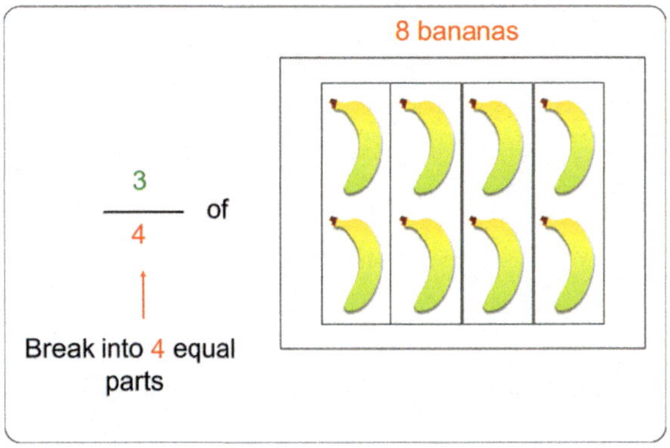

Step 3: Decode the meaning of number 3. It is an encoded instruction: take 3 of the 4 equal groups (shaded to identify them) then count all the bananas in the 3 groups:

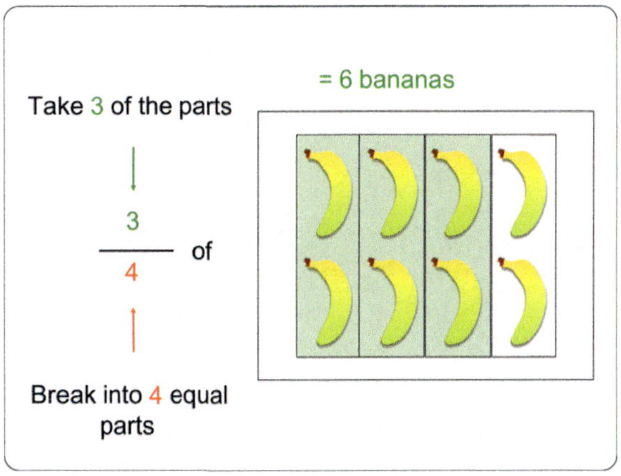

Answer: "Three quarters of 8 bananas equals 6 bananas." This entire sentence can be encoded as a mathematical statement:

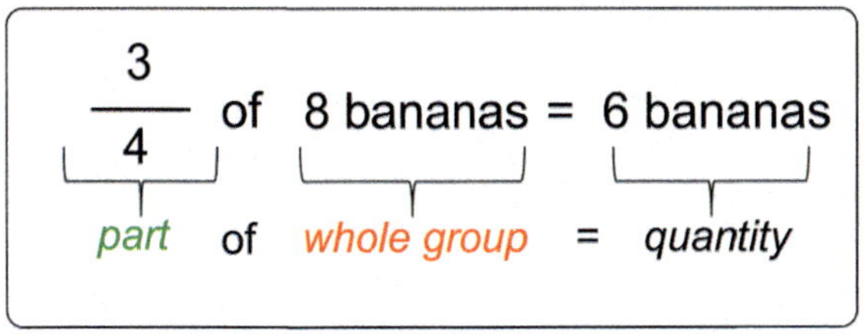

We finally arrive at the first turning point in learning the most fundamental Fraction concept. Before making the turn it is important to realise that by now we are working out, conceptually, how much a part of a given quantity amounts to.

Here is a question: How much is *"three fifths of £10?"*

This can be written using a standard ***mathematical statement*** template like the one shown at the bottom of the frame below (note how the verbal statement is reversed: "3/5 of 10 is how much?"

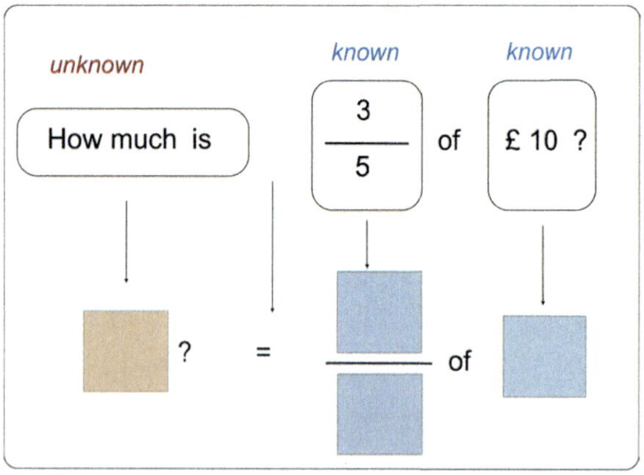

A standard template

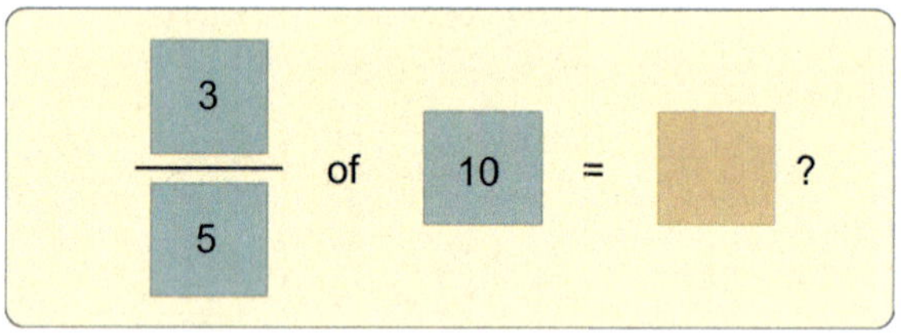

Here are two more questions:

1. How much is "two thirds of 9 kg?"

   Fill in the knowns on the left of "=" sign. The unknown should be asked for, on the right side of the = sign:

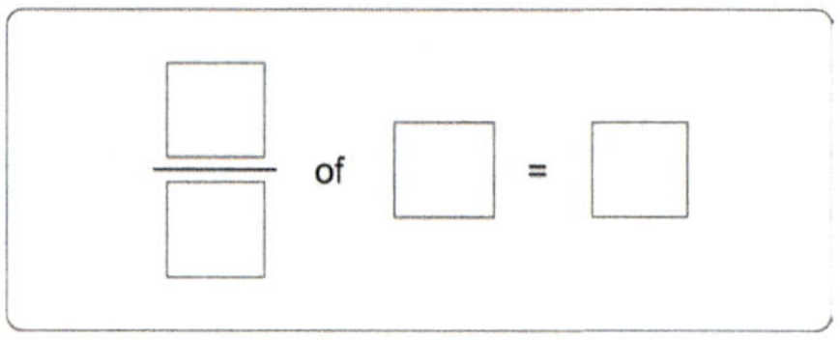

2. How much is " three fourths of 12 km?"

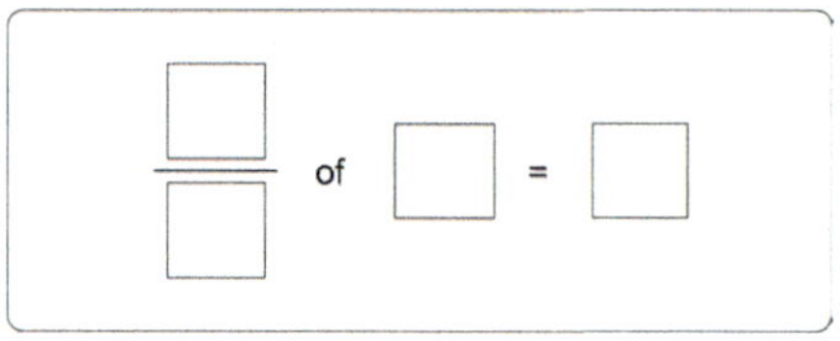

Use your conceptual understanding to decode the meaning of the fractions, then work out the answers.

[The answers are: 6 kg and 9 km]

C. The Mastery Threshold

Mastery at this level requires first-time learners to practice decoding encoded fraction concepts mentally, in different ways, from different perspectives until something "clicks." Often it leads to insights that help learners to negotiate Stages 3 and 4.

For instance, finding the missing information in this template may be easier to do since the large group from which a fraction is being taken, is known (= 12 items in green):

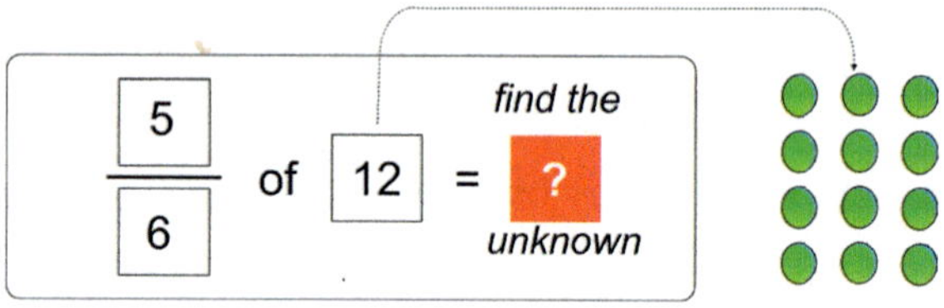

A careful, systematic process of decoding should begin with:

(a) Question: How many smaller groups will you "BREAK" the large group of 12 into? Answer: The BREAK of 6 below the line says to break it into 6 smaller equal groups.

(b) If you have a pencil, you can draw a line around each of the 6 smaller groups. Question: How many will there be in each group? Answer: 2 in each group.

(c) Question: How many of these groups in b) will you "TAKE"? Answer: 5 of them.

(d) Question: So 5/6 of 12 = How many? Answer: 10.

(Count the total number of lemons contained in the 5 groups and you have your answer).

[A] After enough practice with this, you may be ready to tackle something more challenging. It does not require any additional knowledge or information other than what is already known to you. Use a pencil and paper for your writing and visuals:

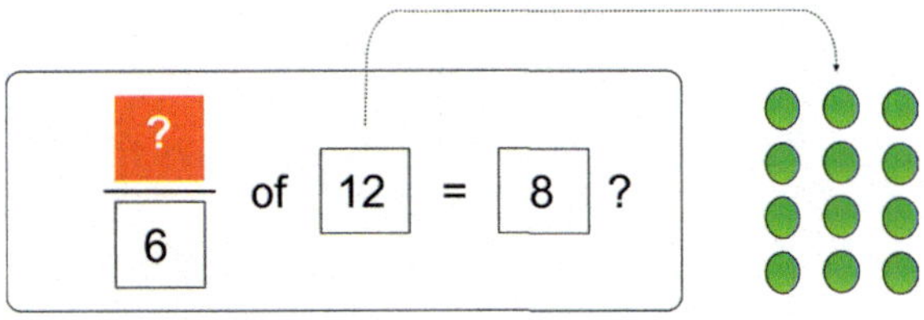

If this template is decoded into words and numbers, it would be like asking:

"I have 12 green lemons. I BREAK them into 6 smaller, equal groups. When I take a certain number (question mark in red box) of those smaller groups, I end up with 8 lemons. How many smaller groups did I TAKE?"

(a) Question: In how many equal groups will you BREAK all the lemons? (known)
(b) After BREAKING them into equal groups, how many lemons will each group contain?
(c) Since you took 8 lemons, how many of the smaller groups did you TAKE to get your 8 lemons?

Answers: (a) 6; (b) 2; (c) 4

[B] Next, let's look for yet another different unknown (shown as a question mark in the red box):

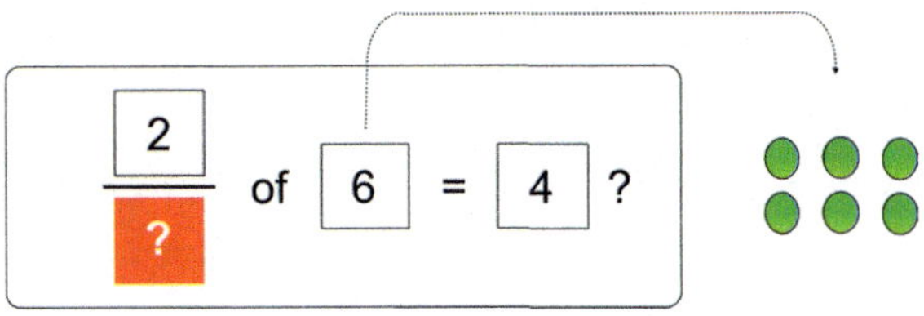

How would you state this problem verbally?

"I have 6 lemons. I BREAK them into smaller groups. When I TAKE 2 of the smaller groups, I end up taking 4 lemons. How many smaller groups did I BREAK my lemons into?"

(a) What is the total number of lemons? (known)
(b) How many melons did you TAKE from the total number of 6 lemons? (known)
(c) How many equal groups will make up the amount you have TAKEN? (known)
(d) How many equal groups will make up the total number of melons?

Answers: (a) 6; (b) 4; (c) 2; (d) 3

Yes, you will pick (d) for your answer. The box in red should show 3.

[C] Finally, try solving this one on your own:

Questions:

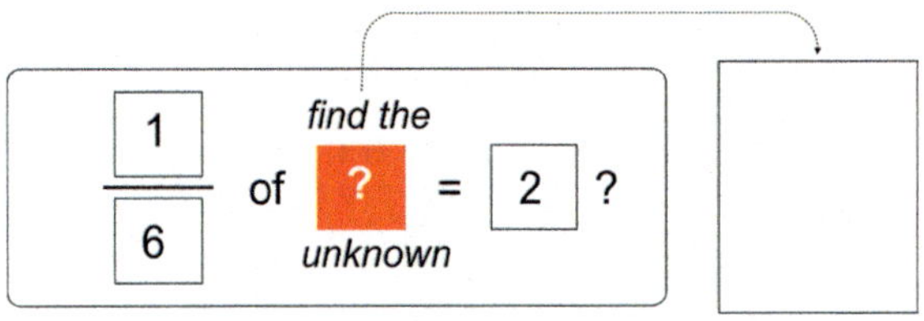

(a) In how many equal groups did you BREAK the total amount?
(b) How many of the groups did you TAKE?
(c) How many are there in the groups you have TAKEN?
(d) How many such groups are there altogether? hint: see (a)
(e) How many items are there altogether (question mark in red)?

Answers: (a) 6; (b) 1; (c) 1; (d) 6; (e) 12

Try drawing all of the above on a sheet of paper as you work your way through them.

A fraction, once encoded, is an entity all its own. Just like a cat which assumes different forms and shapes when sleeping, running, leaping, or lifting it paw. Once we encode the animal as belonging to the cat family, we will recognise it, regardless of its changing postures. Even better, if one is shown a picture of a cat with some part missing, we are able to identify what it is, where it is located and what it looks like. It is because we register the core idea, its essential centrality. It is important to approach fractions by registering its core essence and encoding it numerically as a complete entity.

ANSWERS: [A] (c); [B] (c); [C] (e)

D. The Division-Fraction Connection

You may recall how halves are shown as fractions:

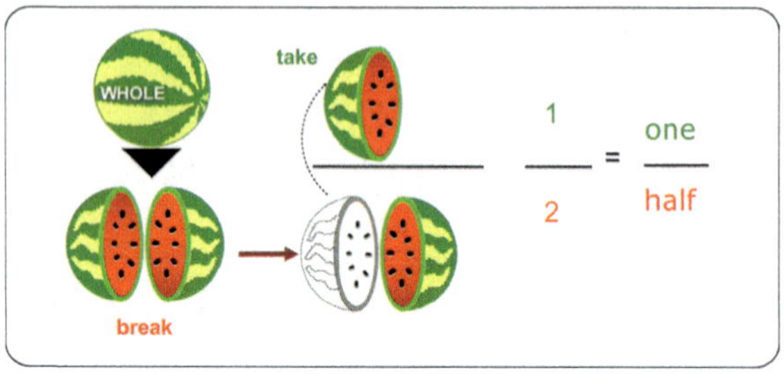

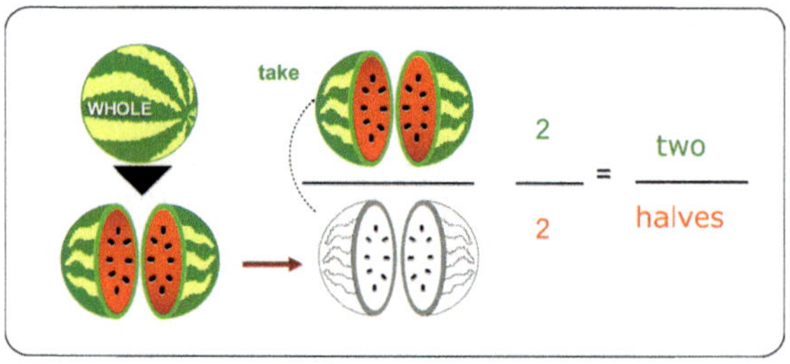

And this is how "Ten Halves" are produced as a Fraction:

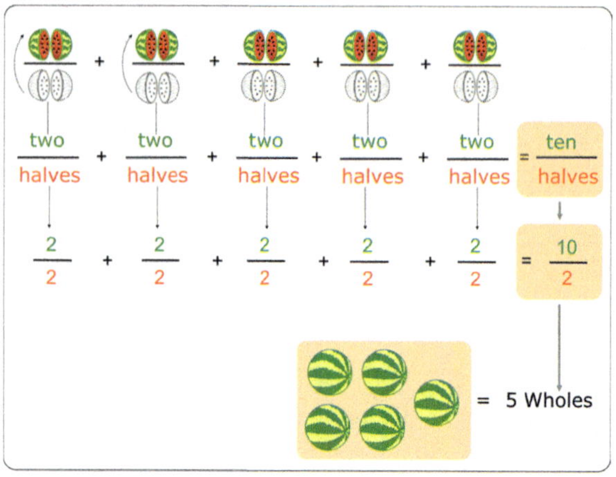

When (2-halves) are added 5 times, repeatedly, it can be expressed as a multiplication statement:

$$5 \times \frac{2}{2} = \frac{10}{2}$$

In short, "**10 halves = 5 wholes**" is written this way in Fractions:

$$\text{10 Halves} = \frac{10}{2} = \text{5 Wholes}$$

To get a perspective on all this, let's look at this code which has been encoded for three different meanings:

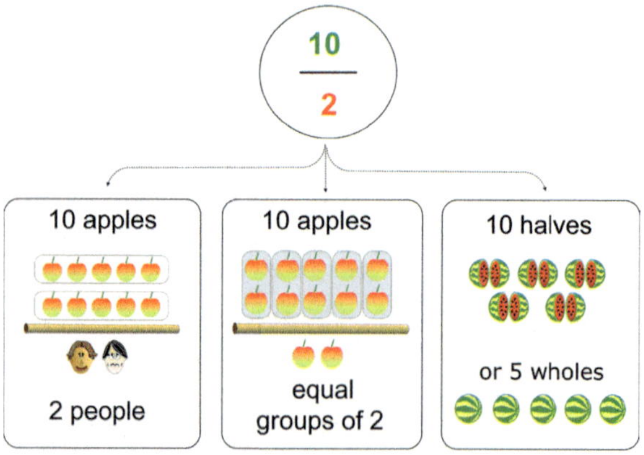

It is important to separate these three mathematical zones, to draw a line around each, as three very distinct mathematical concepts: (a) Division as Equal Sharing (b) Division as Equal Grouping and (c) Fractions.

The first should be mastered before introducing the second. Likewise, mastery of the second will enable a better understanding of Fractions. Achieving mastery is like a tower-building exercise in which the blocks are cemented with mathematical reasoning. The first tower should stand on very sound foundations. It should be supple enough to bend but not break. The same applies to other concepts that enter through the same fraction-symbol, but bring a very different set of numerical reasoning and rules. The learning towers should be so solid that they cannot be nudged or budged by the presence of distracting similarities. This should result in greater clarity. Learners will be able to converge upon the appropriate decoding needed to understand the mathematical context.

Encoding the Concept of Ratio

When things are shared equally, it feels fair. It is intuitive and stands to reason. However, if you worked for 6 hours and I worked for 3 hours, should we both be paid equally? No.

Suppose it took you 9 years to become a doctor. You spent thousands of dollars to qualify as a practitioner while I spent far less time, money and energy to learn to be a brick-layer. Should we be paid the same amount of money for an hour's work?

Or you and I invested in a business. You invested 3 times more money than I did. When we start earning a profit, how should the profit be shared? Should we share the profit equally between us? Would that be fair? Wouldn't it be fair for you to earn 3 times more than myself?

When it comes to sharing unequally, the equal sharing in division doesn't serve us well where unequal sharing is much fairer.. Unequal sharing can take two forms. It could be *2 more*:

e.g. if John earns \$5 an hour,
Jane earns \$5 **+ 2** = \$7 an hour.

It could be 2 *times more*:

e.g. If John earns \$5 an hour,
Jane earns **2 ×** \$5 = \$10 an hour

In the second case, 2 *times more* works like a rate. Both John and Jane's hourly rate (or amount earned per hour) is different and can be stated as a rule, such as:

For every \$5 that John gets, Jane gets \$10.

The word RATIO comes from the word RATE. Ratio establishes the rate for unequal sharing. It is very different from division where a dividing rod makes the division sign (top frame below).

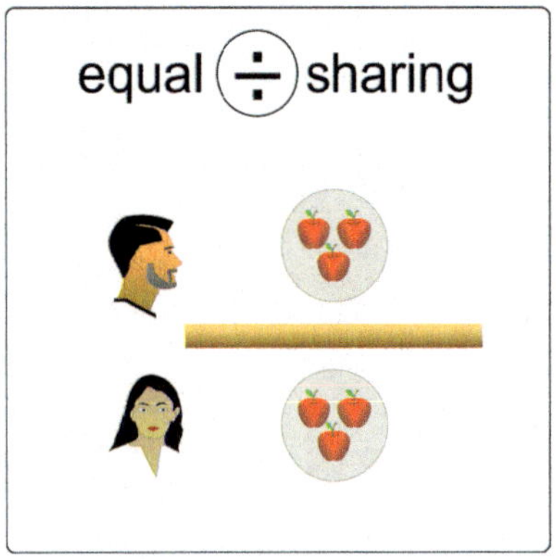

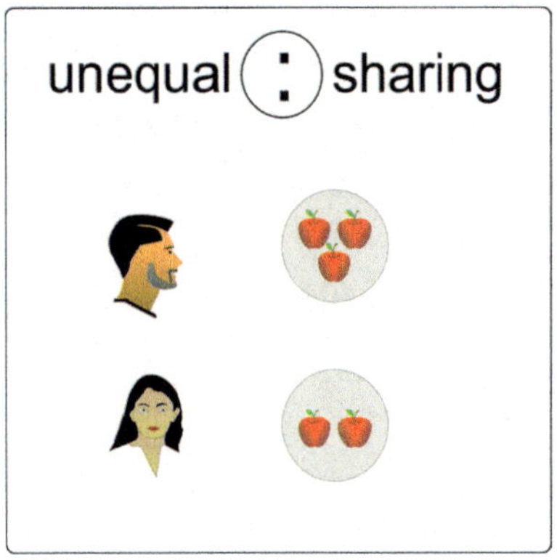

By contrast, in the bottom right frame above, the ratio symbol, is ———> :

There is no dividing rod, just the two dots one above the other to suggest the rate at which amounts are shared unequally. Thus, in the bottom right frame above 5 apples are being shared unequally: one gets 3 apples, and the other gets 2.

When Ben and Sal divide 8 bottles of jam equally between themselves it is shown this way:

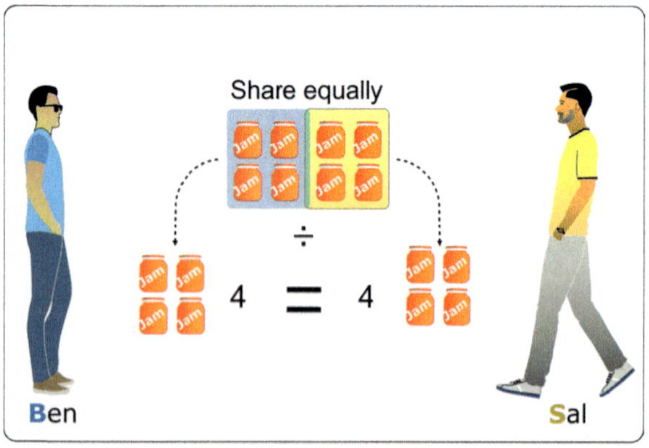

When they share it unequally according to the ratio 3 : 5, it means this:

Sharing rule ratio is 3 : 5

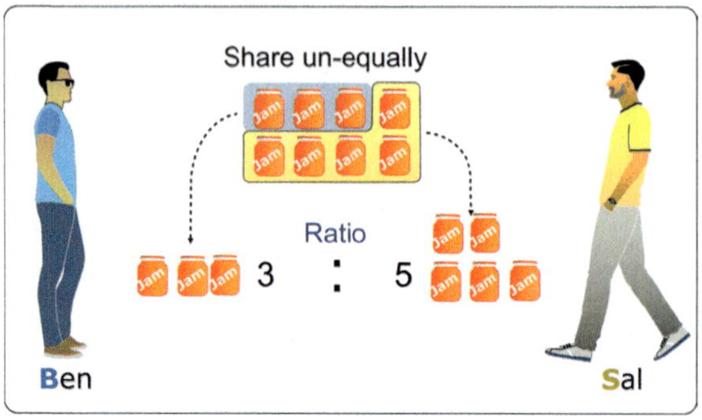

Ben and Sal shared a certain amount of jam in such a way that for every 3 jars that Ben took, Sal took 5. This rule is encoded as:

Ben : Sal
3 : 5

Ayesha and Roxy bought some strawberries. Since Roxy paid more for them than Ayesha, they agreed to split it among themselves by following a simple rule:

"For every **3** strawberries that I get," Ayesha said to Roxy "you get **5**"

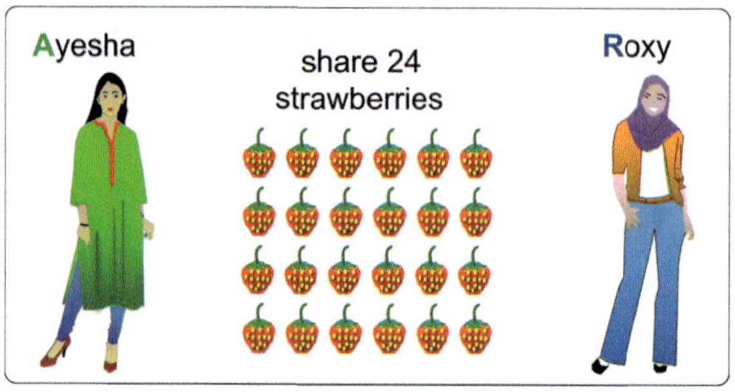

This rule was encoded this way:

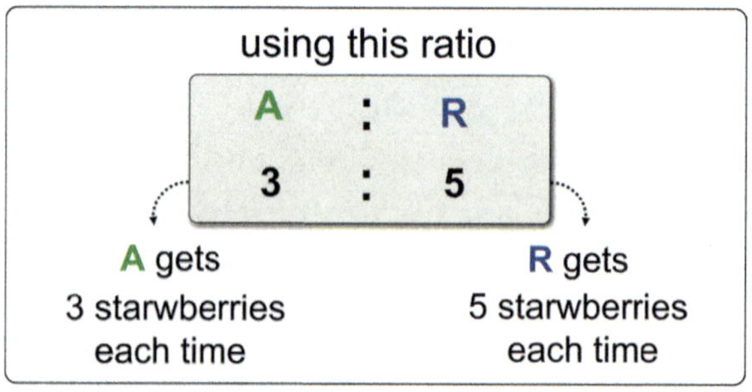

It can also be encoded in reverse this way (it means the same as above):

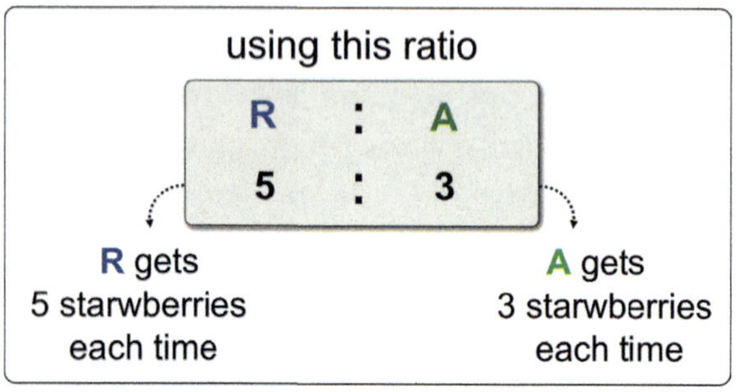

Following this ratio, this is how they shared the strawberries between themselves:

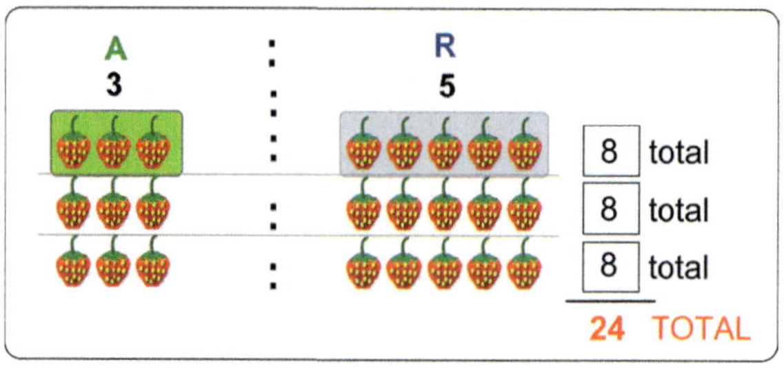

Turn i: First Ayesha took 3 strawberries, Roxy took 5 (see top row, of the bottom frame). So 8 strawberries were shared.

Turn ii: Then Ayesha took 3 again and Roxy took 5 again (see middle middle row of the bottom frame). So another 8 strawberries were shared. But 8 more remained.

Turn iii: So once again, Ayesha took 3 strawberries, and Roxy took 5 (see bottom row of the bottom frame).

Altogether, 24 strawberries were shared between them, where Ayesha received 9 and Roxy, 15. This is shown below:

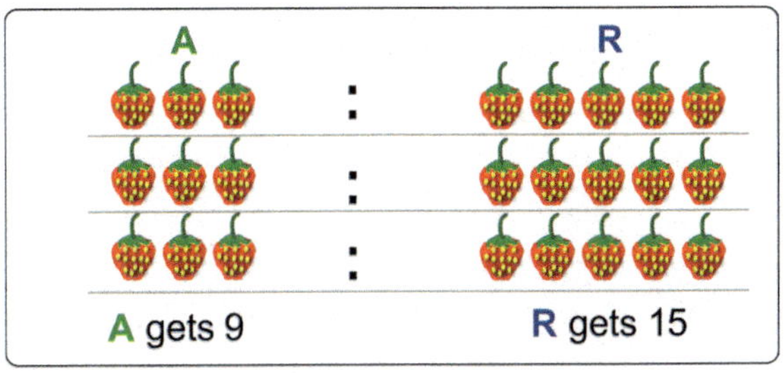

They shared all their strawberries in three turns. At each turn, 8 strawberries were shared altogether, as shown below:

During each turn, Ayesha took 3 of the 8 strawberries and Roxy took 5 of the 8 strawberries. We can express each share as a part of the total number of strawberries in each row of 8. Thus Ayesha gets 3/8 and Roxy gets 5/8:

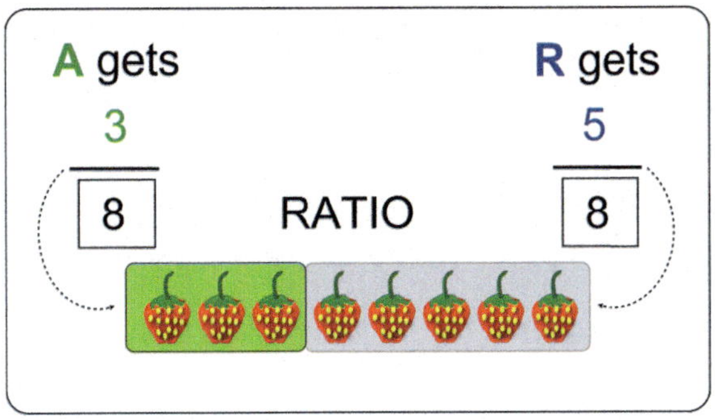

Below we can see how Ayesha and Roxy's unequal sharing of shares is encoded as a ratio:

A : R
3 : 5

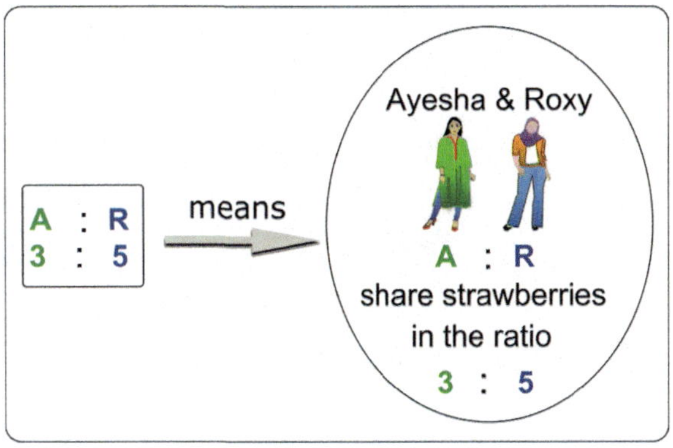

The fraction of strawberries that each gets has also been encoded this way. When we add how much each got (3 and 5), we get the total number of parts they shared between themselves. Ayesha's share is 3 out of 3 + 5 parts, and Roxy's share is 5 out of 3 + 5 parts, as shown below:

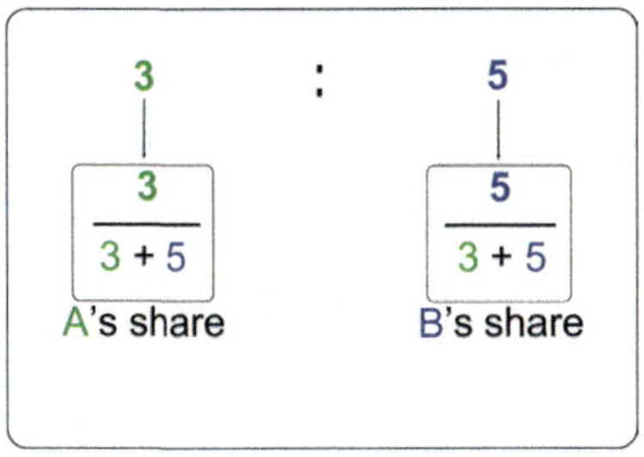

Or:

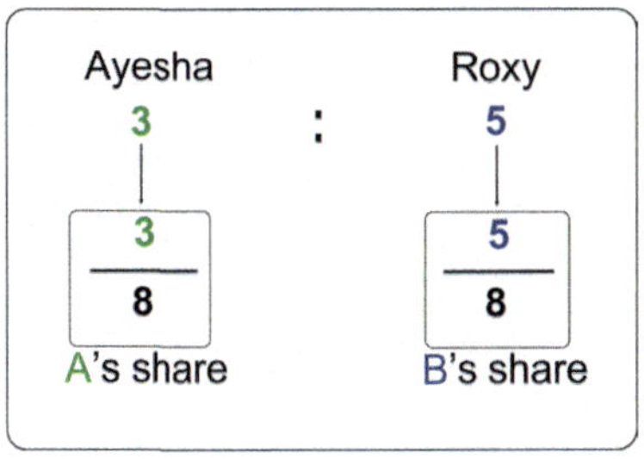

Earlier we saw that a total of 24 strawberries were shared between them in the ratio 3 : 5. This suggests that the 24 strawberries were broken into 8 equal groups, each containing 3 strawberries (shown below). Ayesha took 3 of the groups (shown in green). Roxy took 5 of those groups.

This means that Ayesha's share (in green) is understood to be 3/8 of all the strawberries:

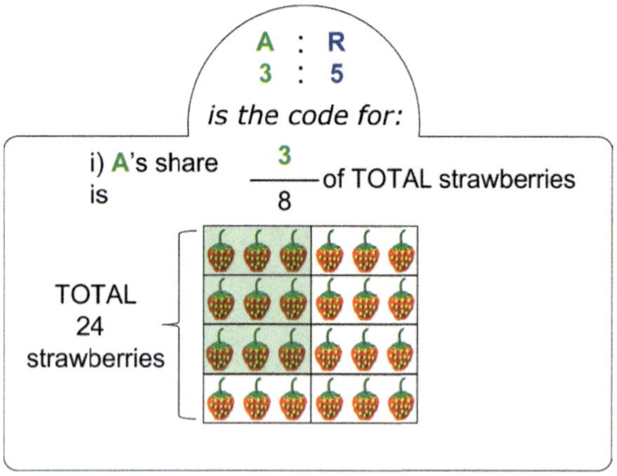

And Roxy's share (in blue) is understood to be 5/8 of all the strawberries:

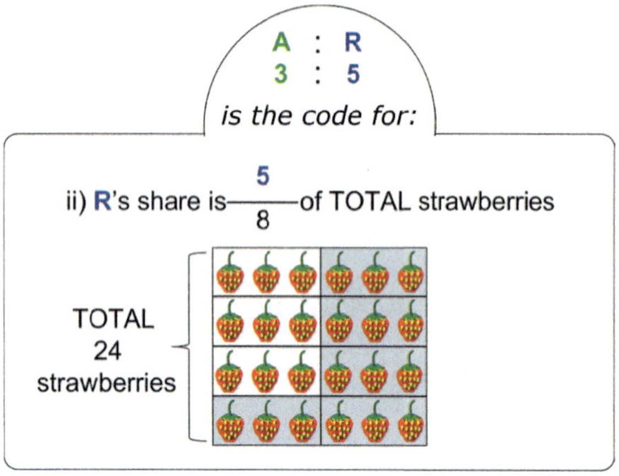

In the end we simply decode the following:

A	:	R
3	:	5

to mean:

i) Ayesha's share is 3 parts out of a total of 8 parts
ii) Roxy's share is 5 parts out of a total of 8 parts

By decoding the encoded (ratio) form in which we expressed unequal sharing, we extracted two meaningful bits of information about how the amount was shared between Ayesha and Roxy.

Why is this so important? Let us sum it up one last time. Imagine for a moment that you and I own a certain amount of wealth. It is tangible, though, and not abstract, i.e. it could be $500 or $1 million, or 100 computers or 3000 horses.

Next, imagine that we agreed to share this wealth in the ratio of 3 : 5:

Me : You
3 : 5

This means that we agreed to break ALL our wealth into 8 (or [3 + 5]) equal shares. Of these 8 shares, I get 3, and you get 5 shares. Or, I will get 3/8 of the total shares, and you will get 5/8 of the total shares.

Now let us return to Ayesha and Roxy's shares and see them one above the other, like this:

If we slide Ayesha's share down so it falls on top of Roxy's share, it will look like this:

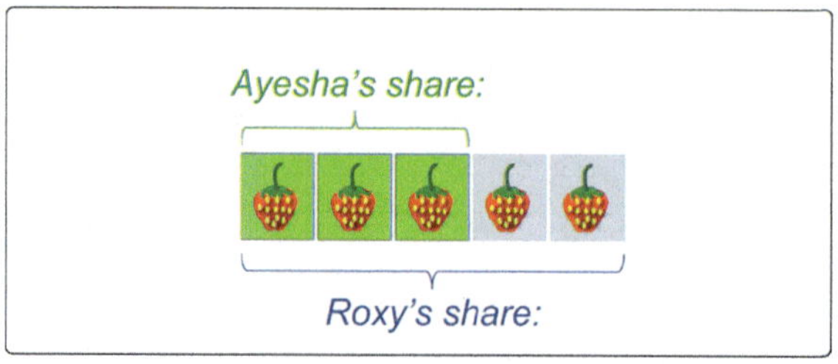

Evidently, out of a total of 5 shares, Ayesha gets 3. This can be expressed this way:

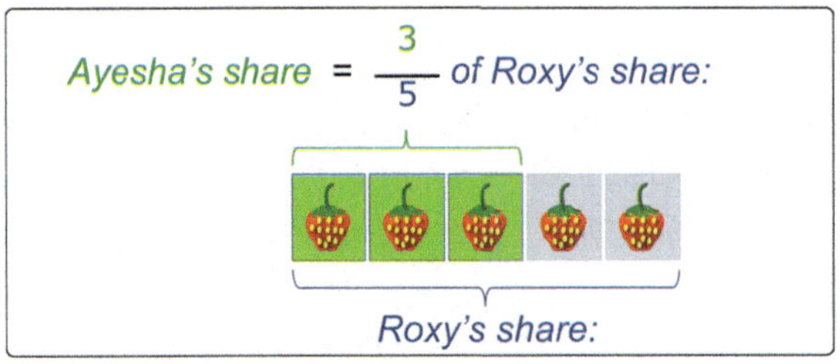

We see now that another bit of information is encoded in the ratio, to read:

iii) Ayesha's share is 3 parts out of Roxy's 5 parts as shown below:

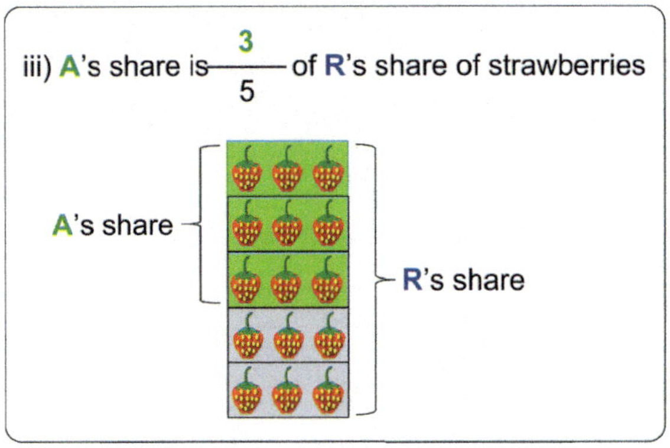

If we apply this ratio to the deal made between us it means:

a) We agreed that you will receive 5 shares of our total wealth of 8 shares
b) And I will receive 3 shares

To express *my shares* ***in terms of*** *your shares*, is like asking:

> *"What part of your share is equal to my share?" Or: "My share = What part of your share?"*

That is the same as asking: "Ayesha's share = What part of Roxy's share?"

We have the answer: "Ayesha's share = 3/5 of Roxy's share"

Here, we expressed Ayesha's share ***in terms of*** Roxy's share. Likewise, *my* share of the wealth will be equal to 3/5 of *your* share.

Altogether, therefore, the ratio code can be decoded to have three meanings:

A : R
3 : 5

is the code for:

i) **A**'s share is $\frac{3}{8}$ of TOTAL strawberries

ii) **R**'s share is $\frac{5}{8}$ of TOTAL strawberries

iii) **A**'s share is $\frac{3}{5}$ of **R**'s share of strawberries

Now try filling in the boxes to test yourself. You and I share a chocolate bar in a certain ratio:

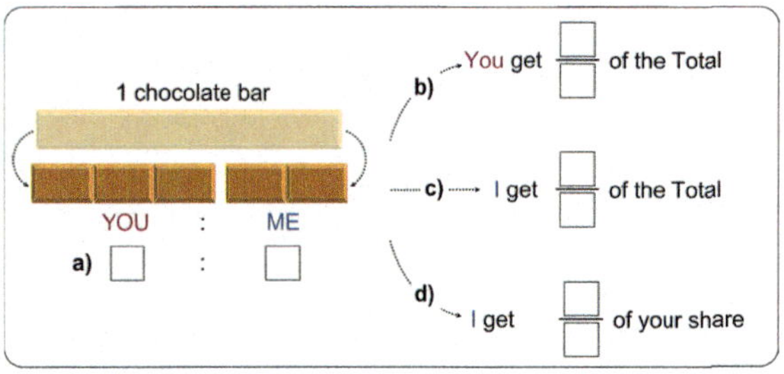

a) What ratio is it being shared in?
b) What fraction of the chocolate will you get?
c) What fraction of the chocolate will I get?
d) What fraction of your share represents my share?

Answers:

a) YOU 3 : ME 2 **b)** $\frac{3}{5}$ **c)** $\frac{2}{5}$ **d)** $\frac{2}{3}$

Here is another example that might secure your understanding of how ratios allot shares. Let us share a bar of chocolate in the ratio 1 : 2. Right away you will see that the bar has to be broken up into 1 + 2 = 3 equal parts first, as shown below:

In the frame below, your share is shown on the left, and my share, on the right.

Notice how it is to be read from left to right, starting with the red print on the left, and ending with the blue print on the right:

"your share (red print) .... is ....
1 over **2** of .... my share (blue print)"

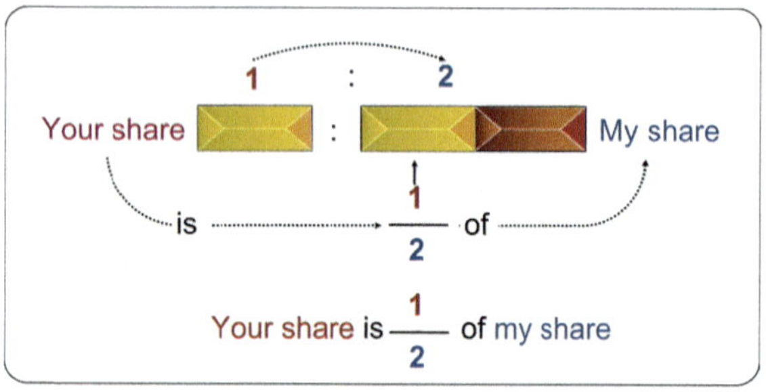

Now read the sentence ***from right to left*** as shown below:

"My share .... is ....
2 over **1** times .... your share"

Notice that this time the numbers 1 and 2 get flipped, as shown below:

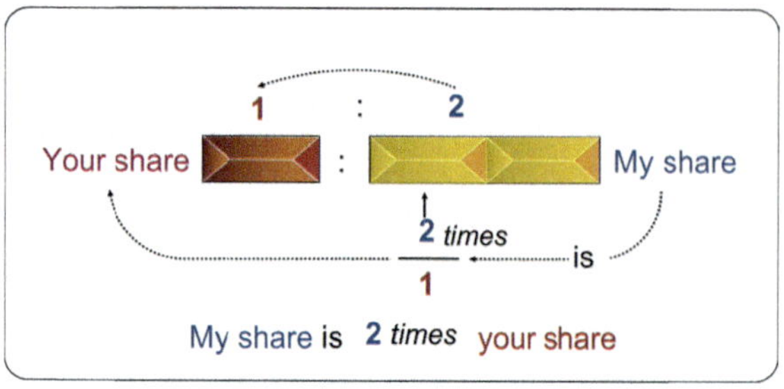

let us share another bar of chocolate in a different ratio, such as, 3 : 2. That means the bar of chocolate has to be broken up into a total of (3 + 2) = 5 equal parts first:

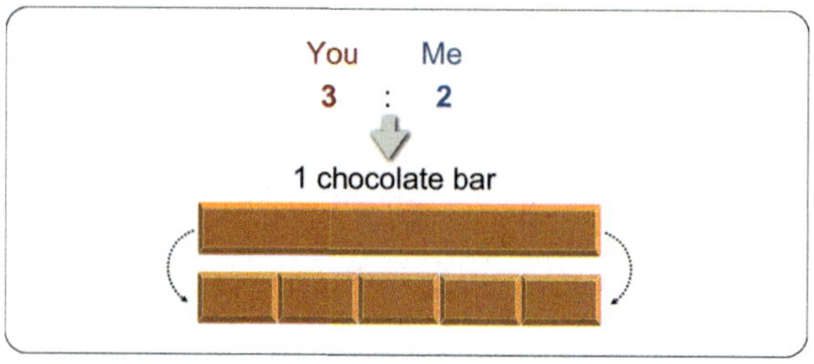

The sharing is shown below for this ratio. This time we will read from right to left first, because we get a very simple fraction ⅔ since we read 2 first, then 3:

"My share .... is ....
⅔ of .... your share"

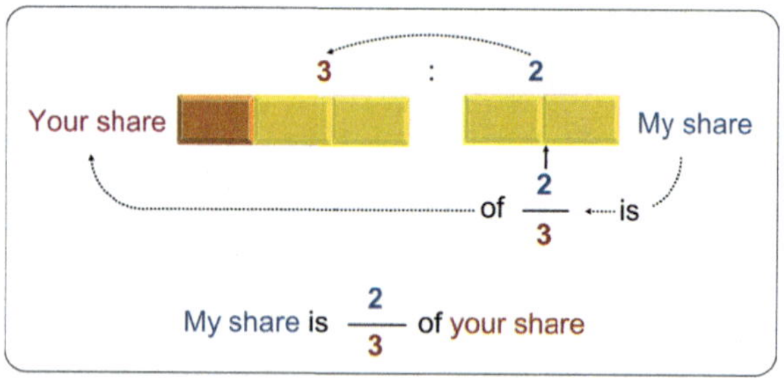

Next we will read ***from left to right*** and flip the fraction ⅔ to 3/2 because we read 3 first then 2:

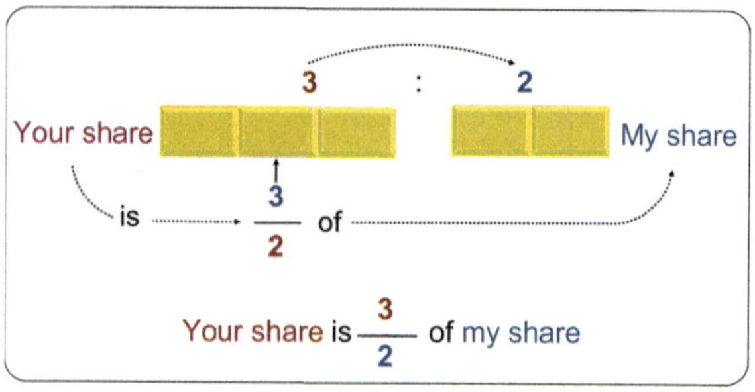

Try decoding the following problem in the same way, then answer the questions that follow:

"Sara checked a recipe for a chicken dish which required two main spices: **C**innamon

and Turmeric; The C and T mixture of 30 gms is made using the ratio:

Cinnamon : Turmeric
2 : 3

Here are the questions:

1) The 30 gm mixture of C and T should be broken into how many equal parts (equal spoonfuls)?
2) How do you express Cinnamon as a fraction of the total mixture?
3) How do you express Turmeric as a fraction of the total mixture?
4) How many grams of the mixture makes just 1 part?
5) How many grams of Cinnamon are in the mixture?
6) How many grams of Turmeric are in the mixture?
7) What fraction of T is C?
8) What if Sara wants to make a mixture of 40 gms instead of 30 gms? How many gms of Turmeric would she need, using the same ratio?

Answers

A 1) the 30 gm mixture can be broken into:

2 parts (Cinnamon) + 3 parts (Tumeric) = 5 parts of the mixture (or spoonfuls) altogether

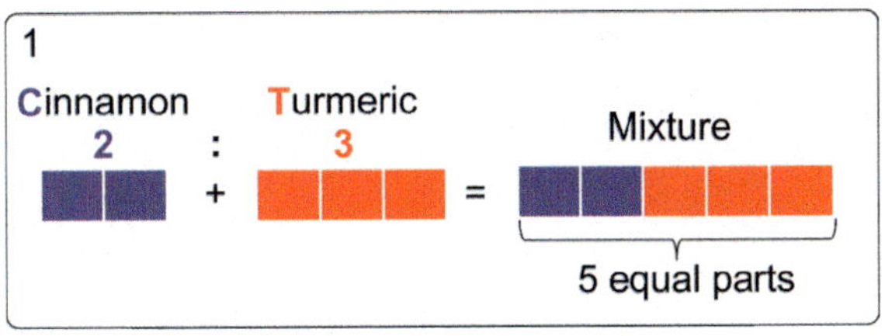

A 2) Cinnamon will be = 2/5 of the whole mixture, i.e. 2 parts out of 5

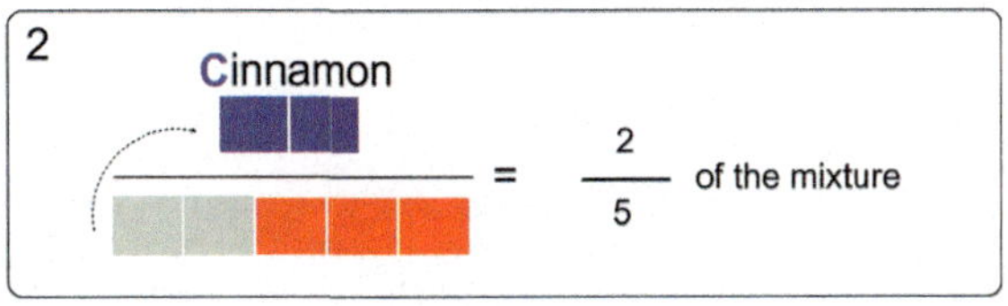

A 3) Turmeric will be = 3/5 of the whole mixture, i.e. 3 parts out of 5

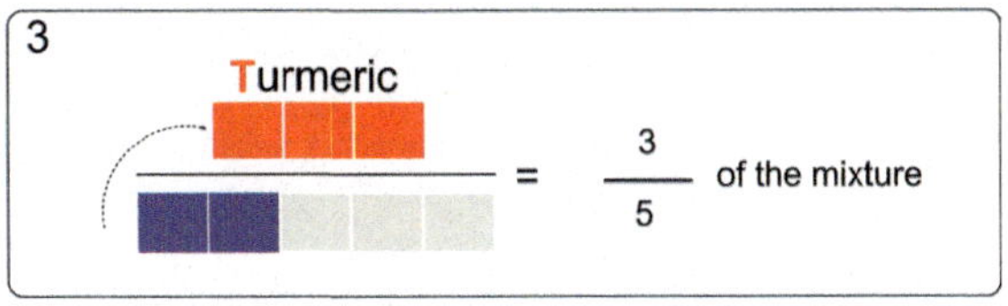

A 4) 5 parts of the mixture = 30 gm. So, each part of the mixture will contain 30 ÷ 5 = 6 gms.

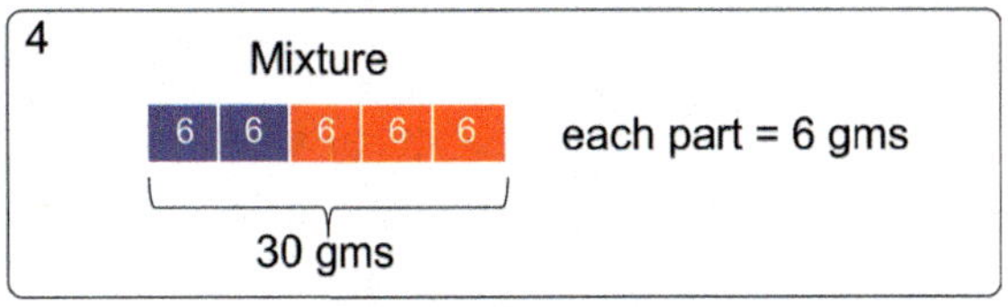

A 5) 2 parts of the mixture are Cinnamon. Since each part of the mixture is 6 gms, the 2 parts are 2 × 6 = 12 gm of Cinnamon

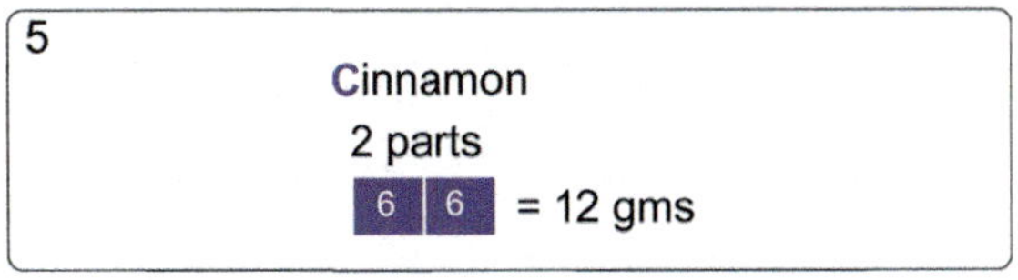

A 6) 3 parts of the mixture are Turmeric. Since each part is 6 gms, the 3 parts are 3 × 6 = 18 gm of Turmeric

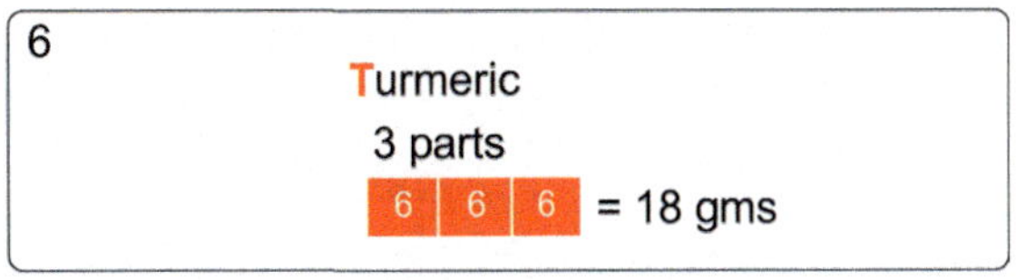

A 7) Cinnamon is 2 parts; Turmeric is 3 parts. That means Cinnamon is 2 / 3 of the Turmeric.

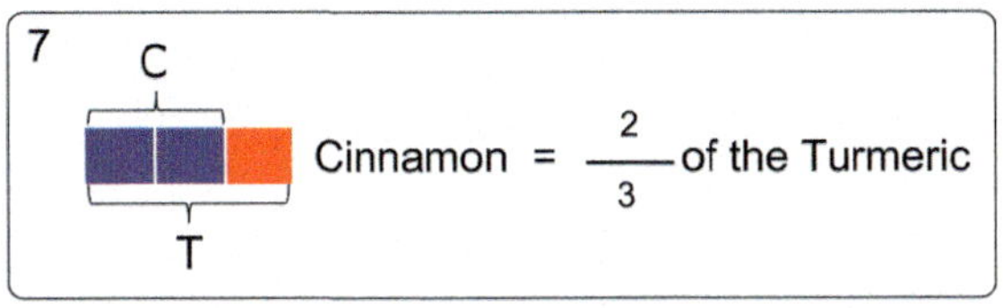

A 8) In this case the 3 + 2 = 5 parts will equal 40 gms so each part would be 40 ÷ 5 = 8 gm.

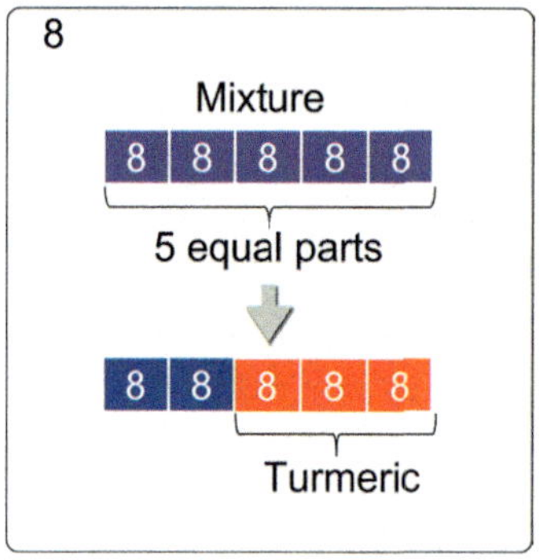

Since Turmeric is made up of 3 parts, Sara will now use 3 × 8 = 24 gms of Turmeric.

A. Expressing Ratio as a Fraction

Often the ratio:

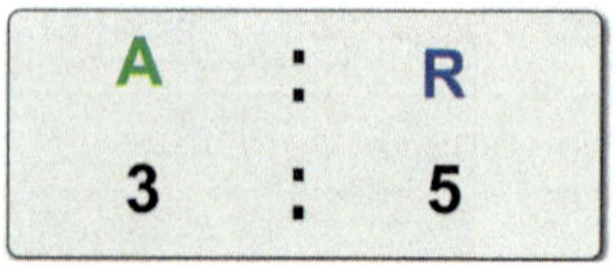

is written as a fraction 3/5:

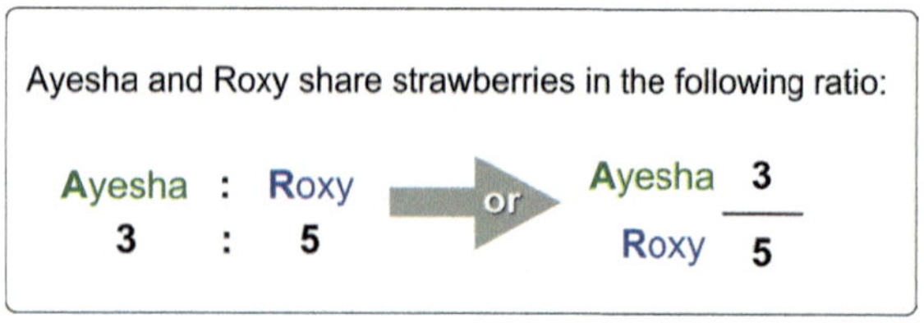

They have to be read vertically for meaning:

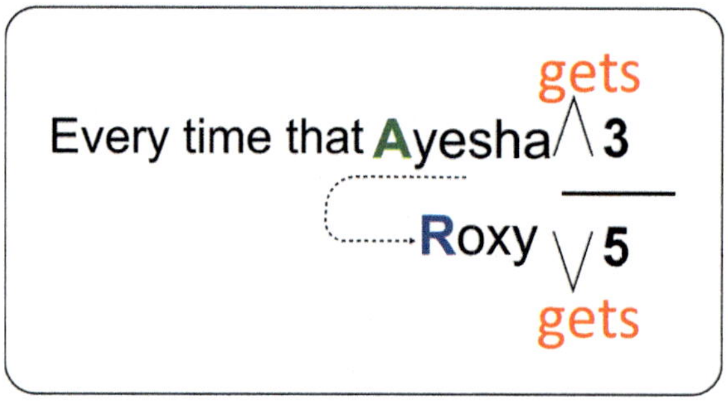

Some people think quite naturally of a fraction as a ratio because it makes more sense to them. For instance, if you were to tell such a person that 5/8 of the cars in the parking lot outside the mall are black, s/he would process it as:

"5 out of every 8 cars are black", or
"there are 5 black cars for every 8 cars"

B. Large and Small Ratios

A higher ratio is one where the difference between the two quantities is very large, or where one quantity is many times larger (or smaller) than the other quantity.

i) For instance, in the ratio 2 : 10 the second number 10, is *five times* bigger than the *first* number 2. It suggests a ***higher*** *ratio (like contrast).*
ii) The ratio 1 : 2 is a much smaller ratio. The bigger number is *just two times* bigger than the smaller number. This suggests a ***medium*** *ratio.*
iii) The ratio 2 : 3 is an even smaller ratio. The second number 3, is *less than twice* bigger than the smaller number 2. It suggests a ***lower*** *ratio.*

Encoding the Concept of Slope in Geometry

Finally, here is another very special kind of a ratio called "slope" ... yes the same everyday slope as in mountain slopes, and sloping roofs, sloping roads, sloping ramps, ski slopes, etc. The concept of "slope" is taught in secondary school when learning Algebra. It has an enormous significance in math.

The house below is shown against a grid. It has sloping roofs.The line and the direction of the left slope is shown in blue:

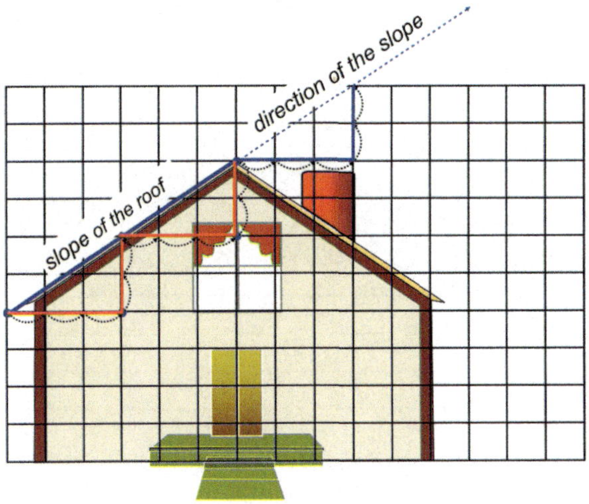

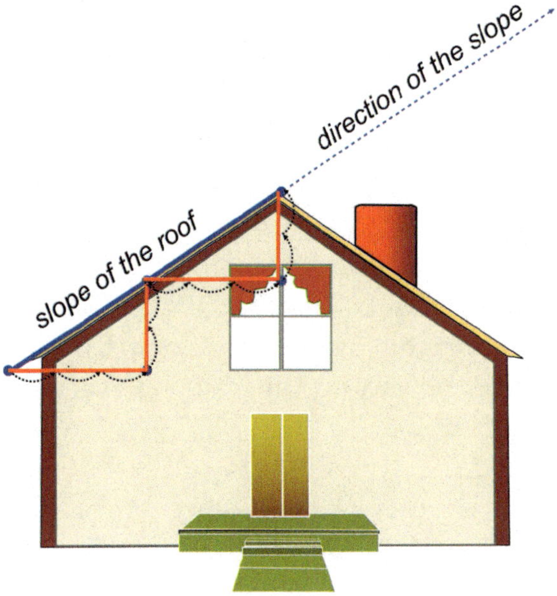

The slope is shown to have two "movements" (in red lines): one is horizontal, from left to right, moving 3 *steps* forward (shown by black arrows in the frame on the right). The other arm is vertical going 2 steps upwards (shown by red arrows in the frame on the right). This pair of movements—3 steps forward and 2 steps upwards each time—determines the direction of the slope.

If you put a ruler on a table and lift up one end at an angle, it will make a slope. If you lay it flat on a grid paper at an angle to the horizontal, it will show a slope.

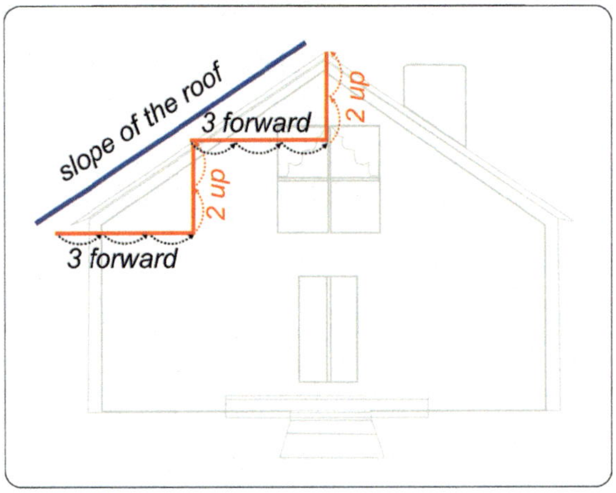

When you draw any straight sloping line on a squared-paper you can draw its slope by first planning two movements, forward and up:

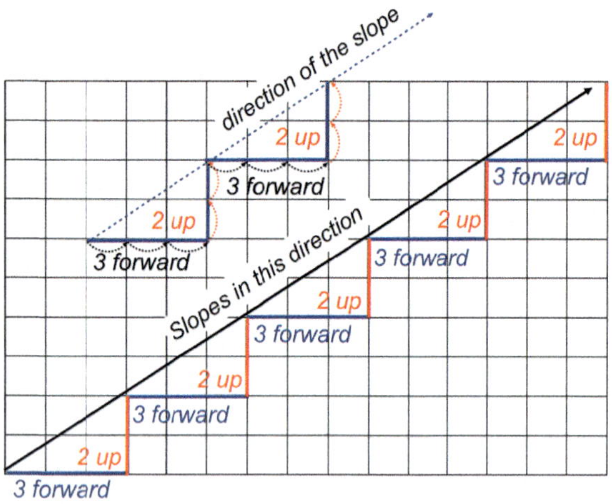

The upward movement is called *"Rise"* since the line rises upwards. The forward movement is called *"Run."* So we can imagine an invisible creature that runs 3 steps forward, then rises 2 steps; runs 3 steps forward and rises 2 steps again; and keeps repeating this pair of movements. It will result in moving in an unchanging direction, along a slope:

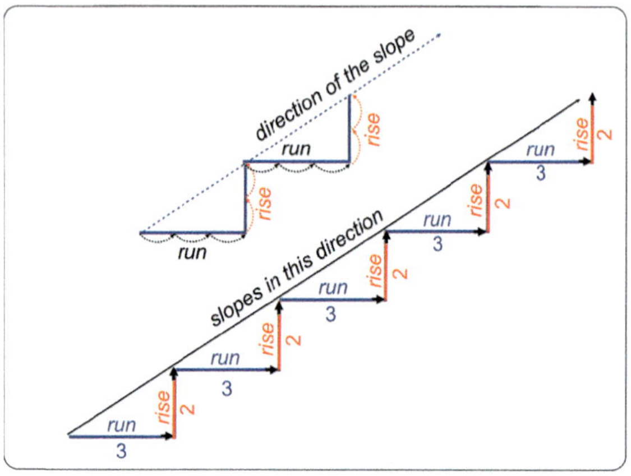

Imagine both the Rise and the Run to be happening simultaneously at the same moment in time. Once a value of Rise (say, 2) and the Run (say, 3) has been locked, the slope remains unchanged, from moment to moment. The slope of a line is defined as ratio of its Rise and its Run. The Rise goes on top and the Run below:

$$\text{slope} = \frac{\text{the height of the Rise}}{\text{the length of the Run}}$$

The definition encodes the concept of the slope and serves as a measure of its size. A steep slope will have a large ratio. A low slope will have a much smaller ratio. The wedge shown below has a slope of 4/10 (4:10)

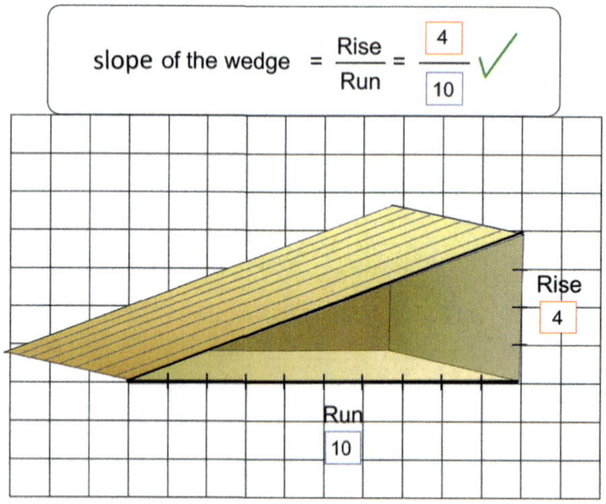

Can you write down the slopes of the lines given below?

Notice that the line with the higher slope, AB, has a larger difference between the Rise and the Run. As a slope increases, the line gets steeper. This is captured by its increasing Rise and decreasing run. The difference between the Rise and Run gets larger. Line GH has a much steeper slope than line JK below.

Which of the lines in the top frames (next page) has the steepest slope? If you look at the value of its slope (written as a fraction) the steepest slope is 4/2 (= 2) for line CD.

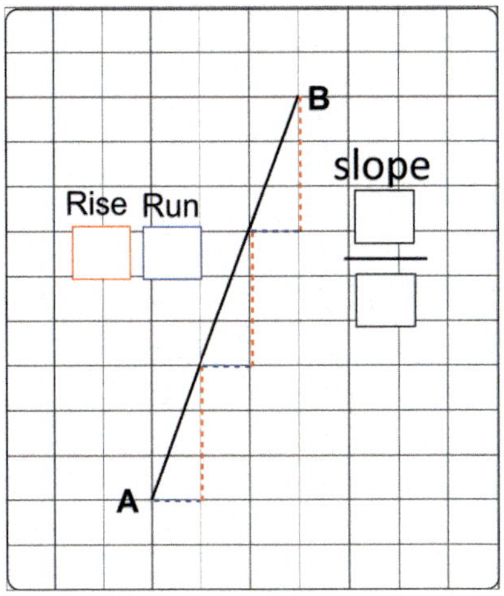

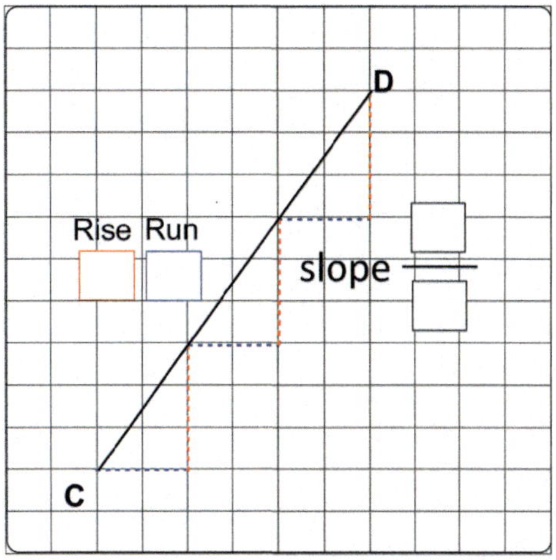

Here are the slopes of three different lines shown below:

$\frac{4}{2}$ $\frac{2}{4}$ $\frac{3}{3}$

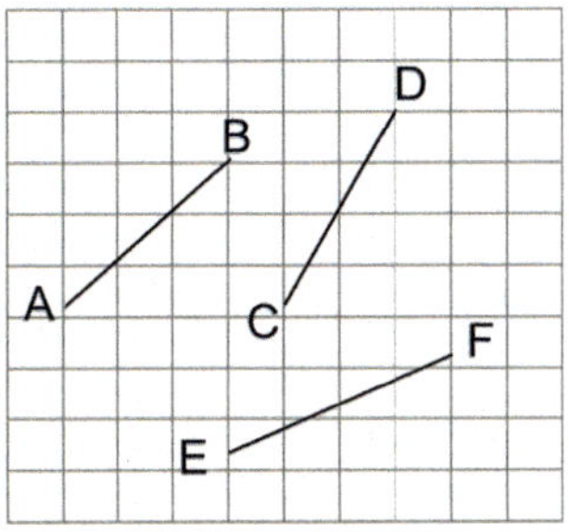

Write down the names of the lines (e.g. line AB) next to each slope:

slope		*line*
$\frac{4}{2}$	⋯⋯→	
$\frac{2}{4}$	⋯⋯→	
$\frac{3}{3}$	⋯⋯→	

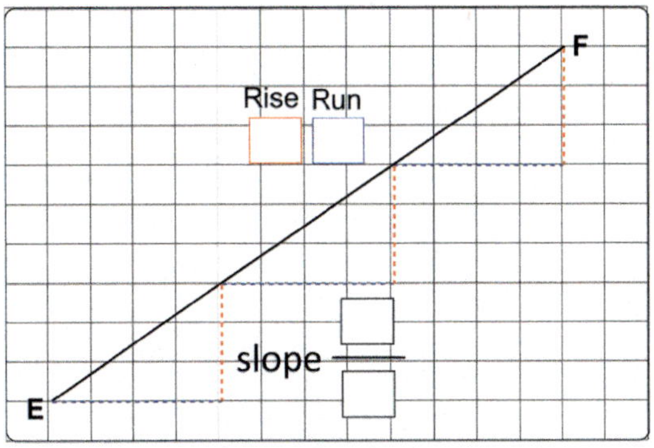

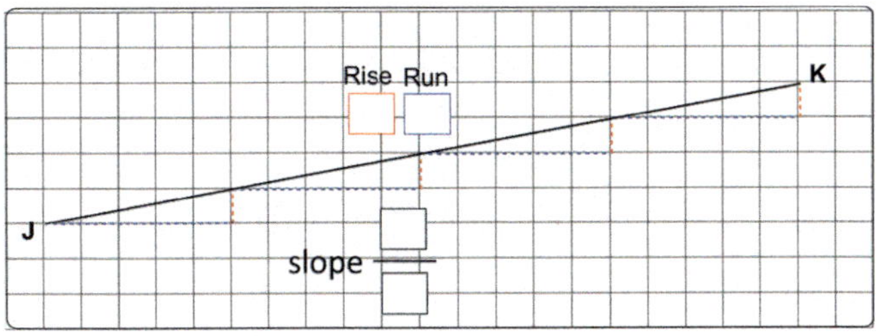

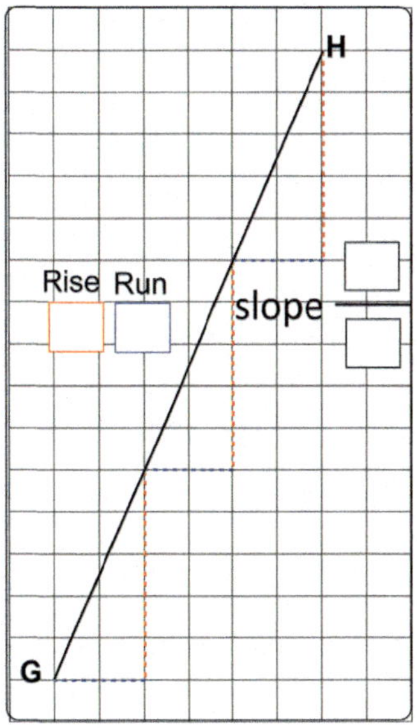

Next, the less-sloping line is AB with a slope 3/3 (**= 1**)

Finally, the least-sloping line is EF with a slope 2/4 (**= Half**)

The mathematical symbol "*m*" for the word "slope" can be best remembered as signifying the letter "m" in "**m**ountain":

For the line AB, *m* = 3/3; line CD, *m* = 4/2 and line EF has *m* = 2/4

The numerical value of the slope decreases as the slope decreases. It is a good way to judge which is the larger fraction. Here are a set of six values for *m*. Draw their Rise and Run (measure in cm) then arrange the fractions from smallest to largest according to their slopes, i.e. from the least sloping to the most sloping:

i) **m** = 2/3 ii) **m** = 3/4 iii) **m** = 4/5
iv) **m** = 2/5 v) **m** = 3/5 and vi) **m** = 5/5

SYMBOLISM 7

Encoding the Decimal Fraction

Our counting system is based on Base 10, which is to say that we count in groups of 10. That's because human civilisation built a number system based on the intuitive impulse to count using 10 fingers. Subsequently, we learned that we can transfer the 10-finger model on to sticks, by making 10 notches on a single stick. So if we have two such sticks we could count up to twenty. If we joined 10 such sticks and made a flat slab, that slab would represent *a hundred*. And when we glue 10 such slabs, surface to surface, we could produce a "block" that represented *a thousand*, and so on. At the base it of all, the number 10 gets repeated: 10 Ones, 10 Tens, 10 Hundreds, 10 Thousands ... and so on.

Counting quantities in whole numbers greater than 1 presented no problem because we developed the Place Value System based on groupings of Tens. The problem that arose subsequently, presented itself as this:

> *How do we count quantities that are made up of* ***smaller parts of a whole****? How do we count amounts that fall between a pair of whole numbers, like between 6 and 7?*

Fractions ... or parts of a room's floor, a piece of paper, of a piece of land, indeed of all solids and liquids....are as much part of our daily life as whole amounts are. How do we measure those parts in terms of how many?

Regular fractions are not enough. For instance, I can draw a piece of land by breaking it up into 10 equal parts. Each part would be 1-*"tenths."* But you may draw it by breaking it up into 16 equal parts. In that case each part would be 1-*sixteenth*. Next we agree to sell a certain amount of the land. I will calculate the area of that amount to be, say, 3-*tenths*. But you would calculate it to be almost 5-*sixteenths*. Comparing your size and mine would get complicated because we will need to find a way to prove mathematically, that my 3-*tenths* is (approximately) equal to your 5-*sixteenths*. Life gets complicated if people start breaking the same amount of land (or anything else)) into different-sized pieces! Think of comparing quantities like the ones below:

$$3\frac{78}{120} \quad \text{or} \quad 3\frac{257}{2000}$$

Which is larger? I broke something into 120 biggish equal pieces but you broke that same thing into 2000 small equal pieces. I took 78 of my biggish pieces. You took 257 of your small pieces. Who received more?

In regular fractions we are free to break a quantity into *any number* of parts we want (like 120 or 2000 above). But this freedom complicates the process of comparing smaller parts.

So the idea of base 10 was extended to smaller parts. In other words, one could break a whole only into 10 equal parts, or 100 equal parts or 1000 equal parts and so on. And each of these smaller parts are called *decimal fractions (deci* [Latin], means *"tenth").* So we can break an amount into **tenths**; or a **tenth** of 10ths which is 100ths) or a **tenth** of 100ths which is 1000ths, and so on.

A. Changing Regular Fractions to Decimal Fractions

Let us look at how the fraction ½ is written as a decimal. Here is a *non-decimal* half:

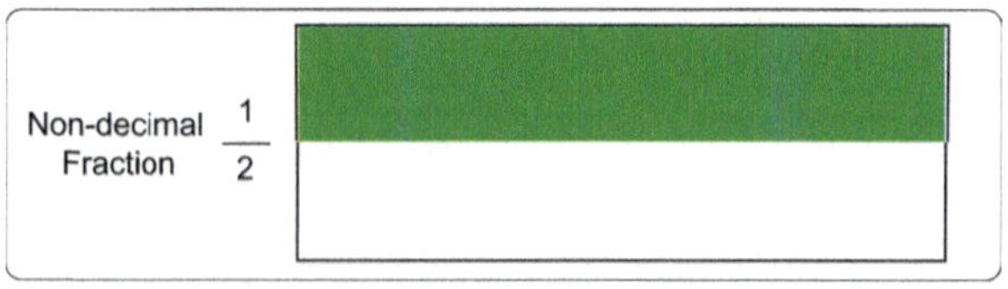

The decimal half requires us to BREAK the whole into 10 equal parts, and TAKE 5:

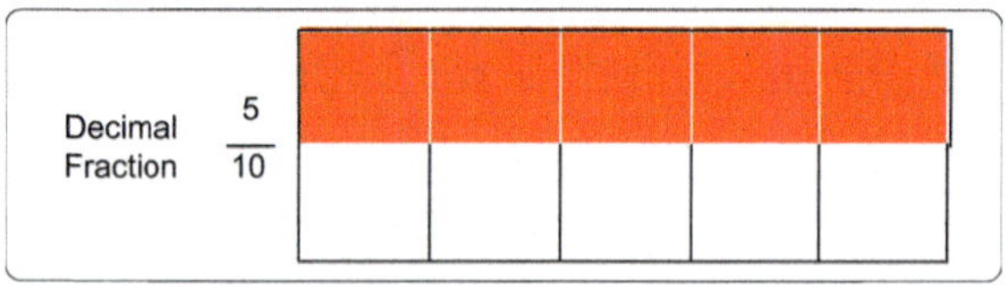

if we TAKE 4 of the tenths it will amount to the green patch below:

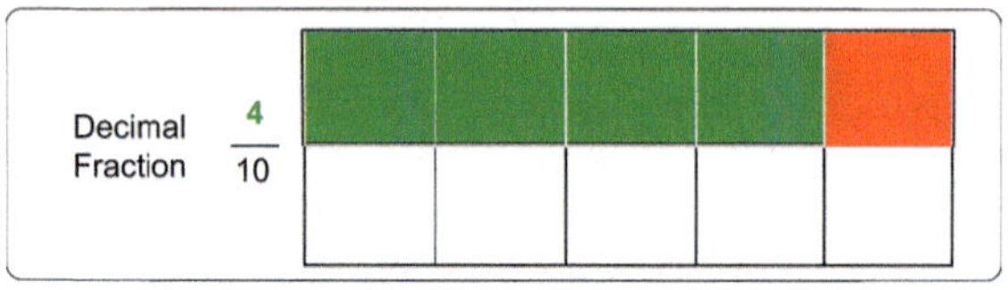

What if we TAKE an amount which falls between 4-*tenth* and 5-*tenth*? That is like saying it falls between 40-*hundredths* and 50-*hundredths*. In that case, let us BREAK each of the 1-*tenths into 10 smaller pieces*:

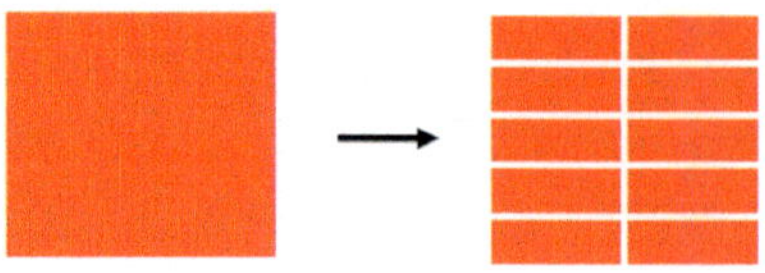

This way the WHOLE now BREAKs into 100 *hundredths*. The ½ is now shown as 50-*hundredths*.

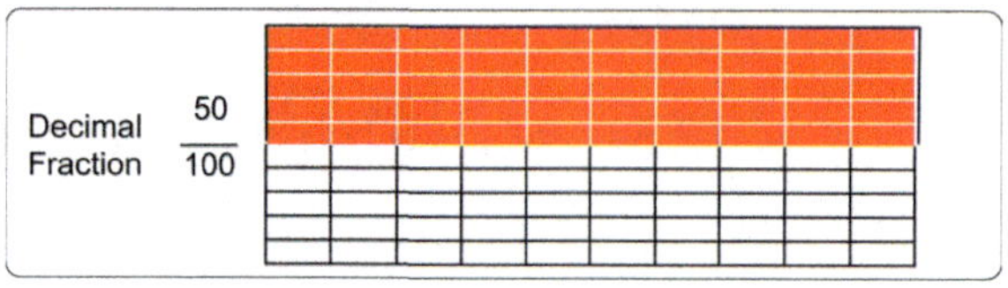

We are now able to TAKE a part somewhere between 40-*hundredth* and 50-*hundredth, e.g.* 45-*hundredth:*

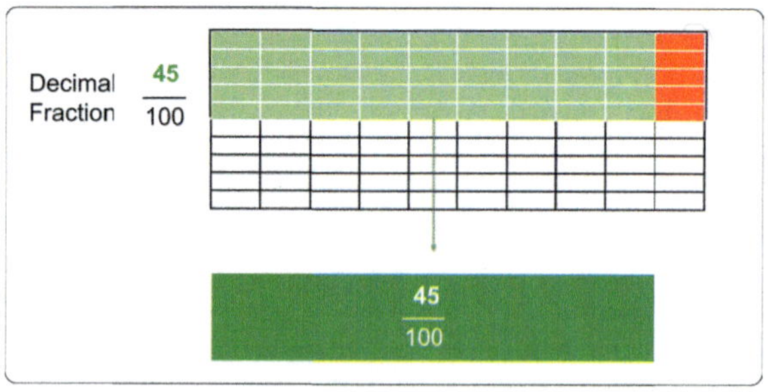

What if the part we want to TAKE lies somewhere between 47-*hundredth* and 48-*hundredth*?

In that case we break each tenth into 10 smaller (but equal) pieces, like this:

That will BREAK the whole into 1000 *thousandths* and ½ will be = 500-*thousandths* as shown below, so *50-hundredths* = *500 thousandths*:

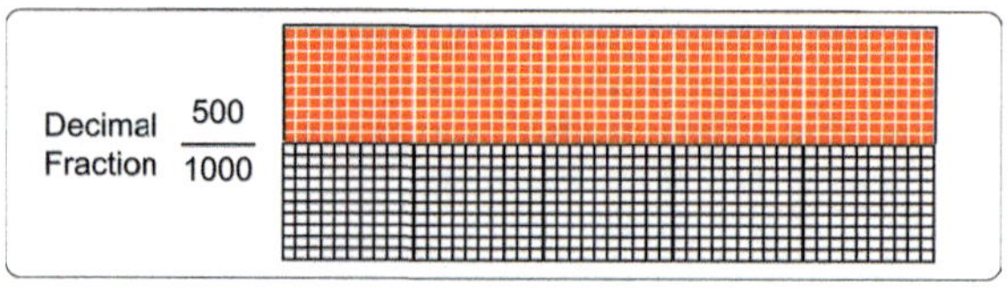

Between 470-*thousandths* and 500-*thousandths*, we have 480-*thousandths*. This is shown in green below:

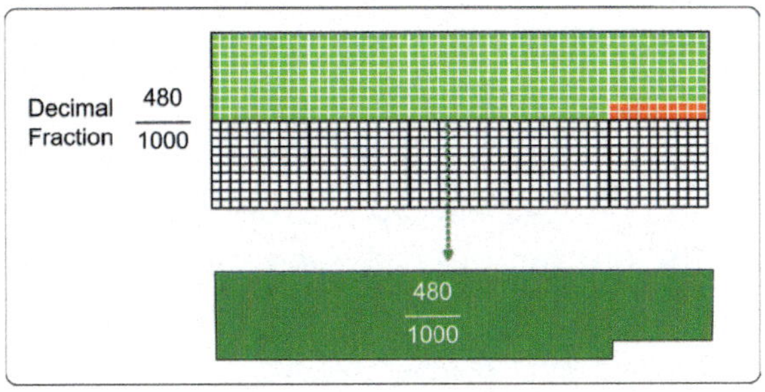

The idea of breaking each part into 10 smaller parts each time makes measurement more and more precise. We can measure things at levels of greater exactitude. In short, we can measure quite exactly, tinier and tinier amounts that lie between whole numbers:

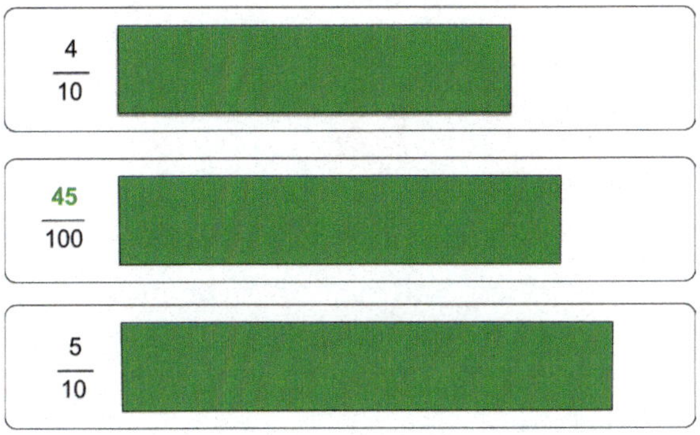

We can also measure amounts that lie between 400-*thousandth* and 500-*thousandth*:

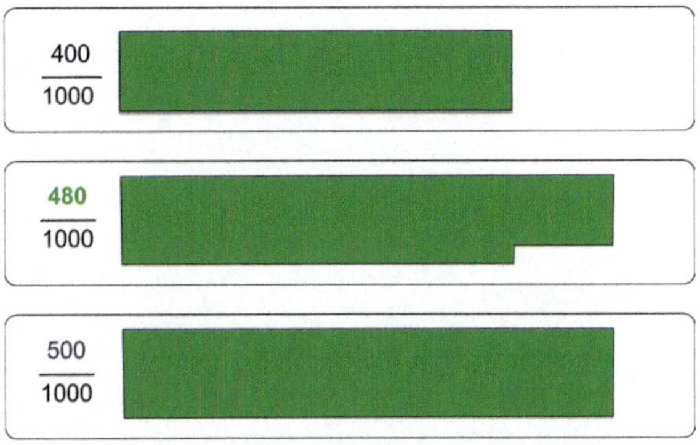

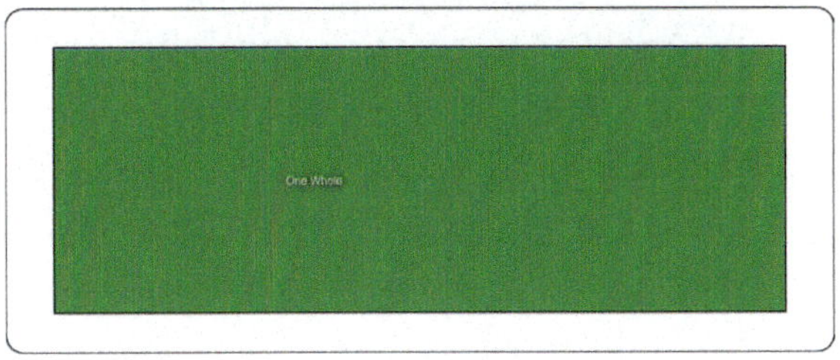

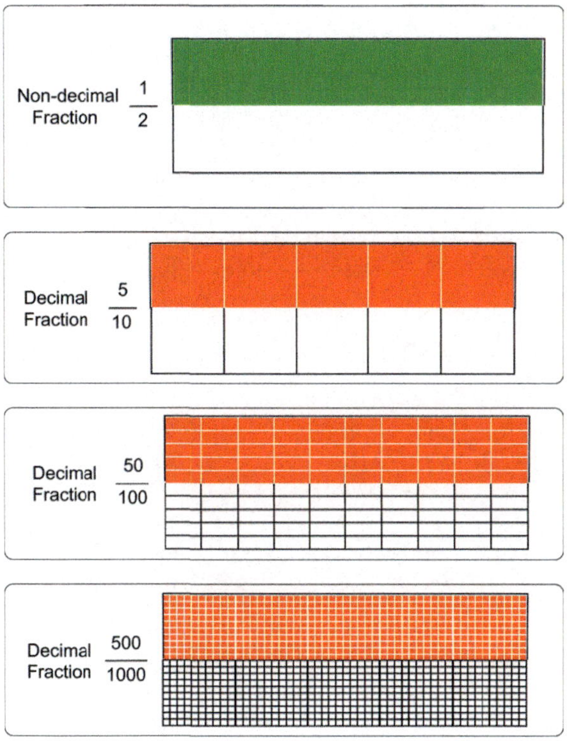

Below you see the many faces of the same Half, as *decimal fractions*:

½ = 5-*tenth*
= 50-*hundredth*
= 500 -*thousandth*

We can show the equivalence of ½ in terms of equal fractions in this way, too:

$$\frac{5}{10} \overset{\times 10}{=} \frac{50}{100} \overset{\times 10}{=} \frac{500}{1000}$$

The sizes of the decimal parts are shown below:

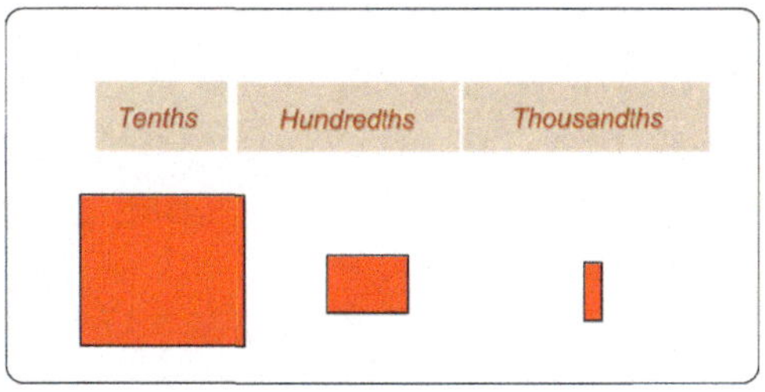

See if you can now recognise the decimal fractions in the set given below:

$\frac{3}{4}$	$\frac{5\,287}{10\,000}$	$\frac{8}{120}$	$\frac{3}{10}$	$\frac{5\,287}{25\,783}$	$\frac{8}{100}$
$\frac{427}{2\,000}$	$\frac{2}{10}$	$\frac{13\,598}{154\,975}$	$\frac{427}{1000}$	$\frac{2}{15}$	$\frac{13\,598}{100\,000}$

ANSWER:

$\frac{3}{4}$	**$\frac{5\,287}{10\,000}$**	$\frac{8}{120}$	**$\frac{3}{10}$**	$\frac{5\,287}{25\,783}$	**$\frac{8}{100}$**
$\frac{427}{2\,000}$	**$\frac{2}{10}$**	$\frac{13\,598}{154\,975}$	**$\frac{427}{1000}$**	$\frac{2}{15}$	**$\frac{13\,598}{100\,000}$**

The template for Place Values is an elegant extension of the counting system that begins with whole numbers (Thousands, Hundreds, Tens, Ones) and extends to the right to show parts that are *smaller than 1 whole* (*Tenths, Hundredths, Thousandths* ... and so on). The *decimal point* (black dot at the centre) separates the Whole Numbers (on its left) from the Parts (on its right):

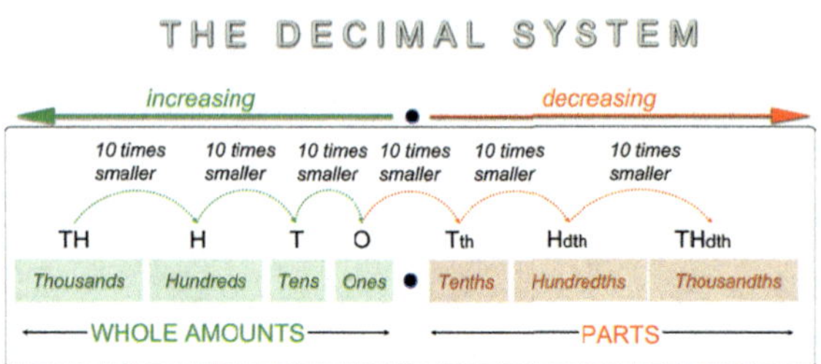

The sizes of the three parts (Tenths, Hundredths and Thousandths) are indicated just below their Place Values:

B. The Decimal Form

The making of a decimal number is no different than the making of whole numbers, shown in the green zone below. Each whole number in 3 627 has its place and each place has its value (3-Th, 6-H, 2-T and 7- O). The making of decimal numbers *less than 1* (or 549 parts of a whole) continues on the right in the red zone, past the *decimal point* which serves as *the separator*. The first decimal is Tenth, followed by a smaller Hundredth, then an even smaller Thousandth and so on. Each is 10 times smaller than the one that precedes it.

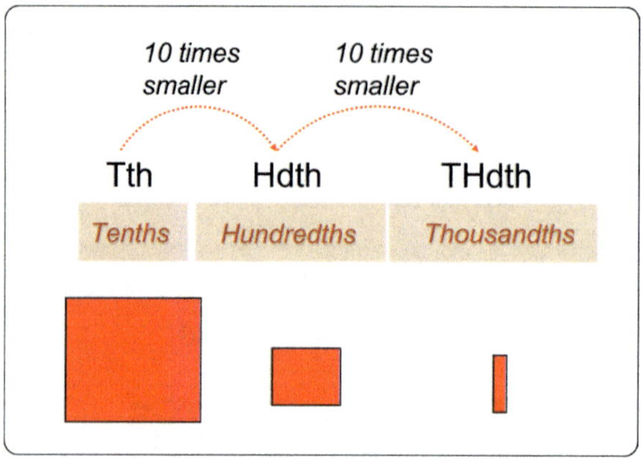

The Place Values for 5, 4 and 9 are shown as:

5-*Tenths* 4-*Hundredths*
and 9-*Thousandths*.

They are written as *decimal fractions* in their appropriate Place Value columns, as shown below:

Making a Decimal Number

WHOLE NUMBERS					PARTS		
TH	H	T	O		Tth	Hdth	THdth
3	6	2	7	•	5	4	9
3000 +	600 +	20 +	7		$\frac{5}{10}$ +	$\frac{4}{100}$ +	$\frac{9}{1000}$

Decimal fractions adopt a certain *form*, an appearance that identifies them as being a *decimal number*. Their unique decimal identity is expressed in the ***decimal form*** as shown below:

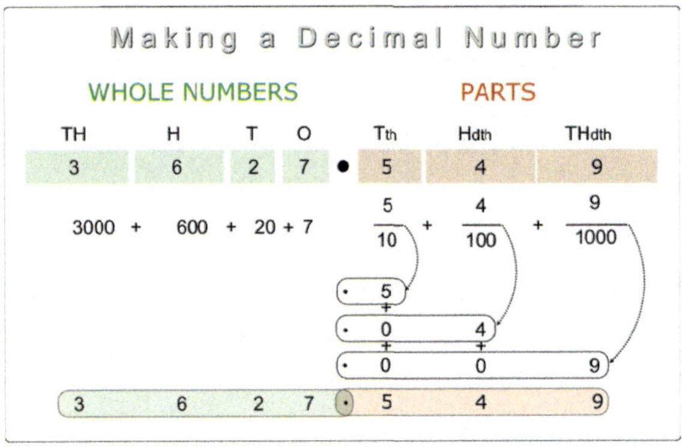

i) Thus, 5-*Tenth* is written as **. 5**
ii) On its right is 4-*Hundredth*, which is written as **. 0 4** The "0" before **4** indicates the absence of a Tenth.
iii) Similarly, 9-*Thousandth* is written as **. 0 0 9** The two "**0 0**"s before **9** indicate the absence of a Tenth *and* Hundredth before it.

Reading the entire number from the green zone to the red zone, from wholes to parts, we have the following completed decimal number written in the *decimal form*:

3 6 2 7 . 5 4 9

This is how to say it aloud in words:

"Three thousand six hundred and twenty-seven ***point five four nine***."

It would be incorrect to read . 5 4 9 as "*five hundred and forty nine*" because their place values have to be respected. 5 is written below "*Hundredth*" not "Hundred." The same circumspection has to be applied to the numbers 4 and 9. (They are *not* "Tens" and "Ones"). They should be read exactly as they are written, in the decimal form, below their Place Values:

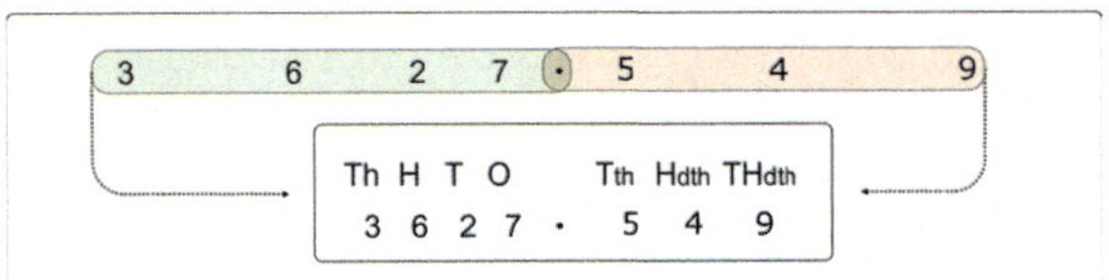

In the frame below, the whole numbers (green column) are written on the left of the *tenths* (pink column), as always in any fraction. The *decimal form* for each mixed number on the left is shown on the right of the equal sign:

Whole Number UNITS	*Decimal Fraction* Tth		*Decimal Form* U • Tth
0	$\frac{5}{10}$	=	0 . 5
2	$\frac{8}{10}$	=	2 . 8
5	$\frac{9}{10}$	=	5 . 9
6	$\frac{2}{10}$	=	6 . 2

When we add the *Hundredths* (grey column) to the *Tenths*, their *decimal form* takes up ***two decimal places***:

Whole Number UNITS	*Decimal Fraction* Tth	*Decimal Fraction* Hth		*Decimal Form* U • Tth Hth
0	$\frac{5}{10}$	$\frac{9}{100}$	=	0 . 5 9
2	$\frac{8}{10}$	$\frac{2}{100}$	=	2 . 8 2
5	$\frac{9}{10}$	$\frac{5}{100}$	=	5 . 9 5
6	$\frac{2}{10}$	$\frac{3}{100}$	=	6 . 2 3

Whole numbers and decimal numbers follow the same rules when they combine to represent a single quantity. For instance, the whole number 259 *(two hundred fifty-nine)* is made this way:

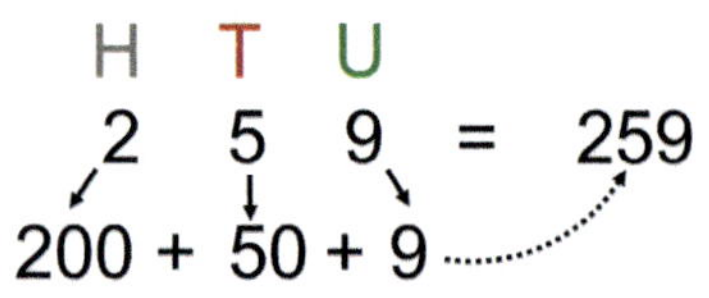

Likewise, we add up two decimal fractions to get the final amount **0.59**:

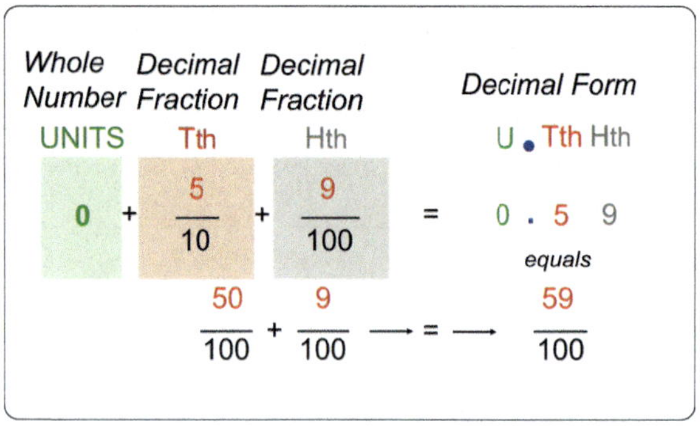

We can see how the decimal fraction equivalent for the decimal form 0.59 is 59-*hundredths:*

$$0.59 = \frac{59}{100}$$

Likewise, we add three decimal fractions to make the decimal 0.597:

$$0.597 = \frac{597}{1000}$$

The frame below shows how the decimal fraction equivalent of 0.597 is 597-*thousandths:*

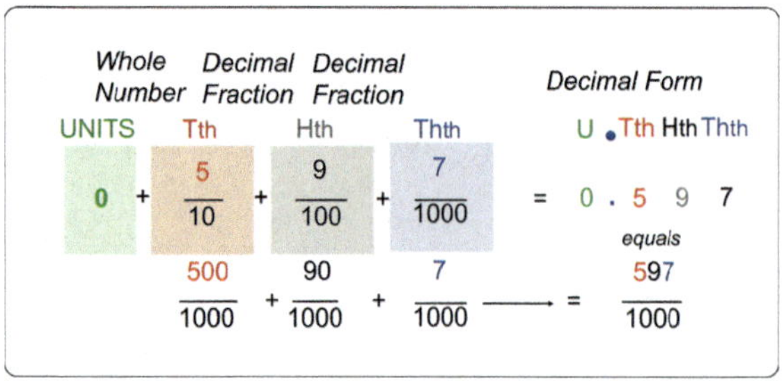

It is worth noting that 9-tenths (or 0.9) is the largest fraction in the "tenth family." Look at 6 wholes and 9-tenths written in the decimal form, 6.9:

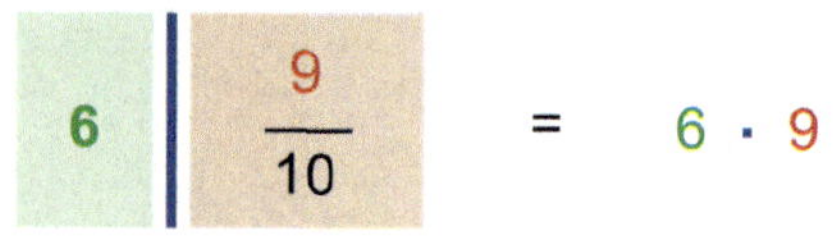

If you add another 10th to 9-*tenth*, it will amount to 10-*tenth* which turns into a single whole unit. This whole unit (1) is added to 6 whole units to become 7-*ones*:

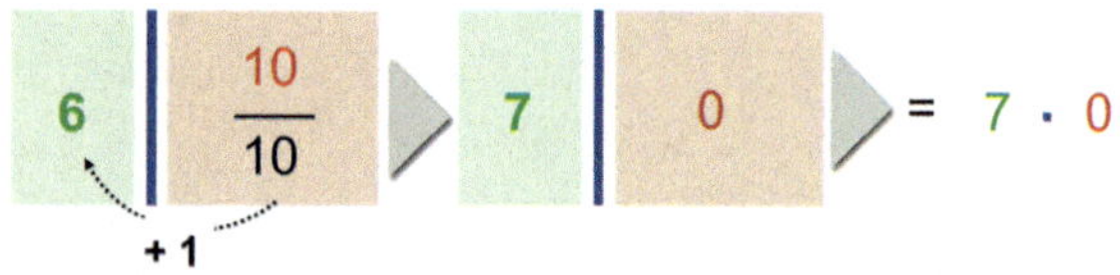

Now try the following exercise. Write the decimal fraction for each mixed number shown as dollars, in whole numbers from a) to e). Each of them is attached to parts (of a single dollar) expressed in *decimal form*:

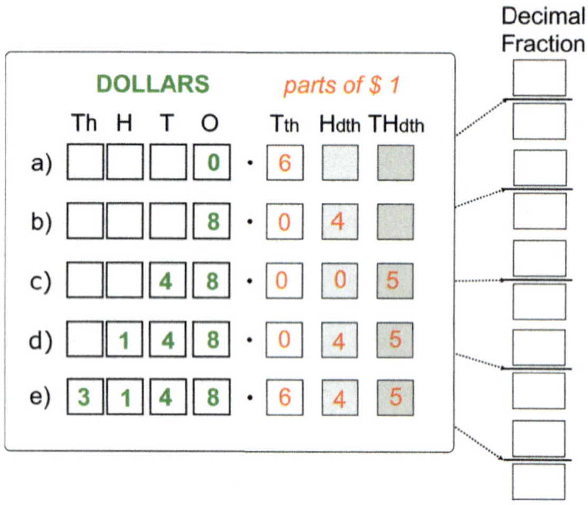

The answers are shown below:

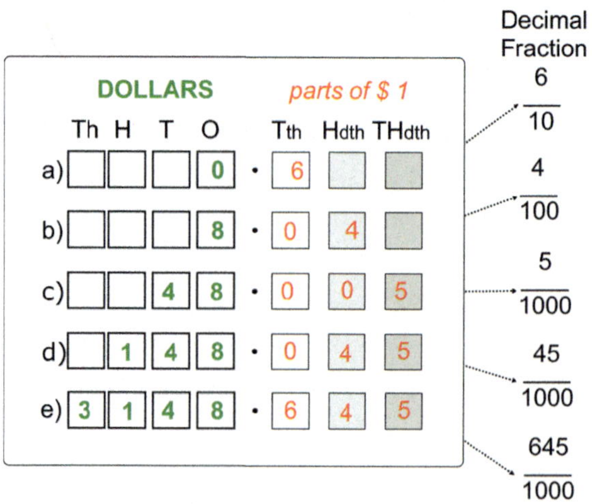

SYMBOLISM 8

Encoding Percentage

The understanding of Part-Whole relationships is a pervasive theme in mathematics.There are aspects of mathematics that require us to test our underlying assumptions about what we understand and compute. In fractions and decimals we are put to test when we practice breaking wholes into smaller parts, then smaller and smaller parts yet again. In decimals we learn the art of measurement with exacting precision. Here too we are tested when practicing to break a whole unit into thousands, millions or billions of minuscule parts.

Achieving exactitude and precision is critical. Today we can, with the aid of powerful magnification tools, correct any error in the measurement of, say, an angle, by a billionth of a degree. A billionth of a degree deviation can create a huge angle of deviation in the trajectory of a space-craft on a three light-years' journey through space. It may end up arriving at another planet!

This is in sharp contrast with the concept of percentage.

In fractions, we had the freedom to break a whole into any ... and indeed, many ... number of randomly created smaller parts. It made comparisons of quantities extremely laborious. For instance, which is bigger: the fraction 28/349 or 412/6007? This will take time to compute. Decimals introduced both ease and discipline. So, which of the two decimal fractions is bigger?: 29/100 or 678/1000? When we write them as 0.29 and 0.678 we can tell at a glance by comparing the size of the first decimal digit in each of the numbers 0.2 and 0.6 (the second one is greater). We can also think of 29/100 (0.29) as 290/1000, then compare this with 678/1000, as Like fractions.

Percentage, in comparison, brings another revolutionary dimension to mathematical thinking. Yet, it is strikingly simple. First let us look at the word "**Percent**age" with two root words originating in Latin. The first is "cent" (see below). Four of the most common words in our vocabulary use the word *cent*, which means *hundred* (or 100):

CENT

Century	**Hundred** years	100
Centennial	**Hundred**th anniversary	100
Centigrade	**Hundred** steps	100
Centenary	**Hundred** years completed	100

In Latin, the word *"per"* means *"for each"* and this is often extended to implicate another meaning: *"out of."* The emergence of the symbol for *per cent as "%"* is shown below:

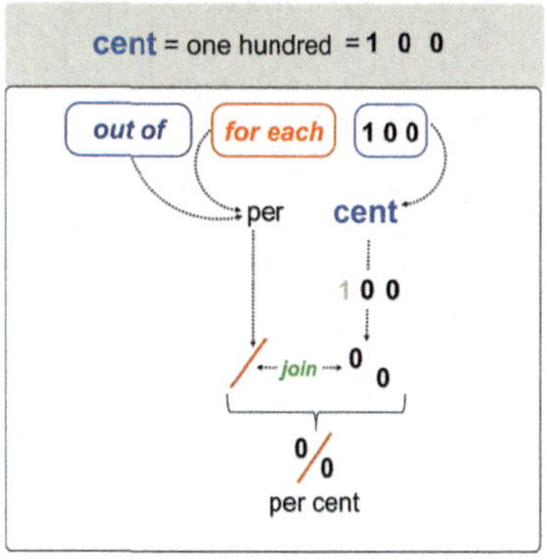

When we say 8% (8 *per cent*), we mean 8 *for each* 100, or 8 *out of* 100. Either way, we write it as: **8%**.

Percentage represents a very special fraction where a whole unit, or a whole amount, is imagined to be broken up into 100 equal parts. It doesn't matter how much, how big, or small that *Whole* amount is. If the whole amount is 1 month, then the month is broken into 100 equal parts. So when we say: **10% of 1 month**, we mean the following (see the Frame in red):

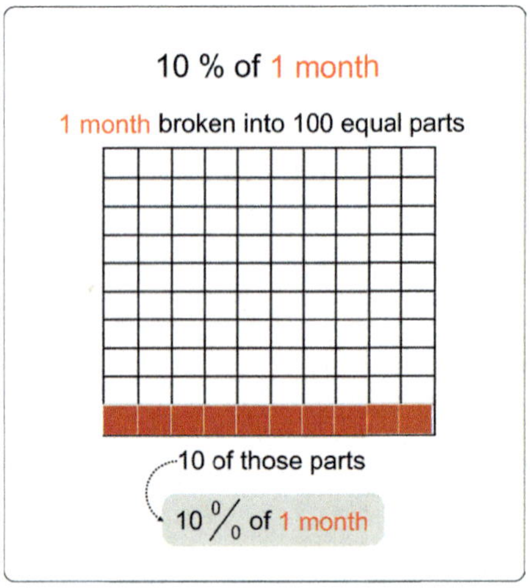

If the Whole Amount is imagined to be $2, then the $2 is broken up into 100 equal parts and **15% of $2** can be shown as (see Frame in green):

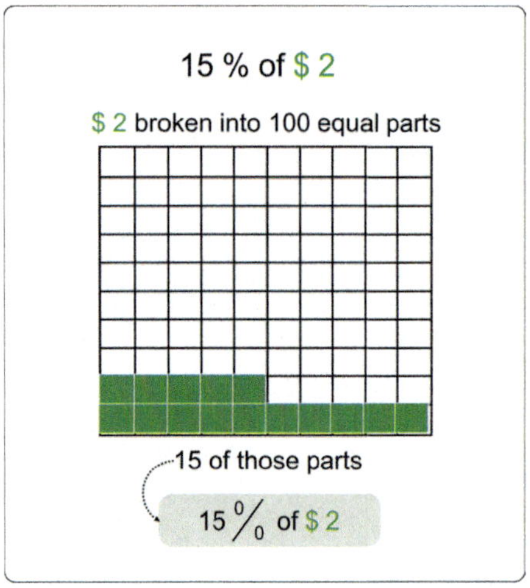

Likewise, if the whole amount is imagined to be 5 pages, then the 5 pages are broken up into 100 equal parts and **30% of 5 pages** can be shown as (Frame in blue):

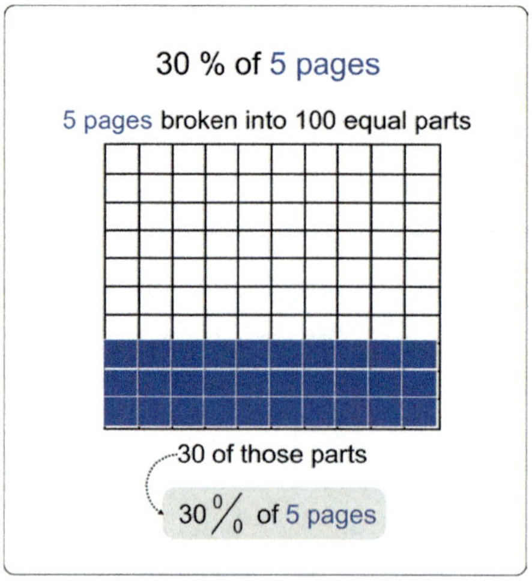

Percentage teaches us, among other things, to imagine all measurable items of any collective magnitude (quantity), as a *single whole*. It can be 1 month or 10 (when measuring time), $2 or $1 million (when measuring money), 5 pages or 500 pages (when measuring the number of pages) 20 Kg or 1000 Kg (when measuring weight).

Below, **55% of 20 Kgs** is being shown as (Frame in purple):

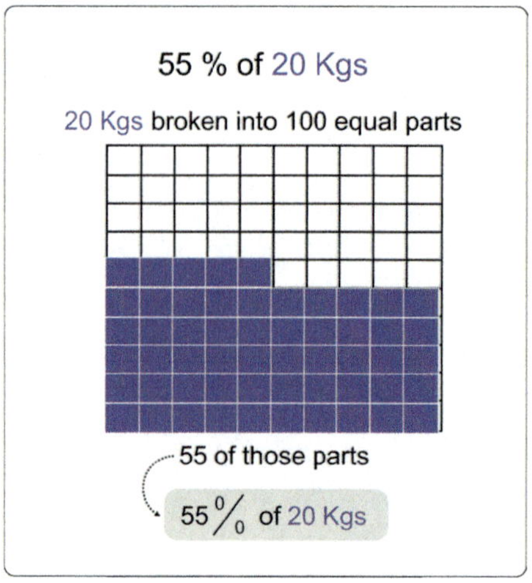

What about an amount *less than 1*, such as a quarter or ¼? How can we express a quarter as *something out of 100*? The answer is obvious: we take ¼ of 100, which is 25. Next, we write 25 out of 100 as **25%**:

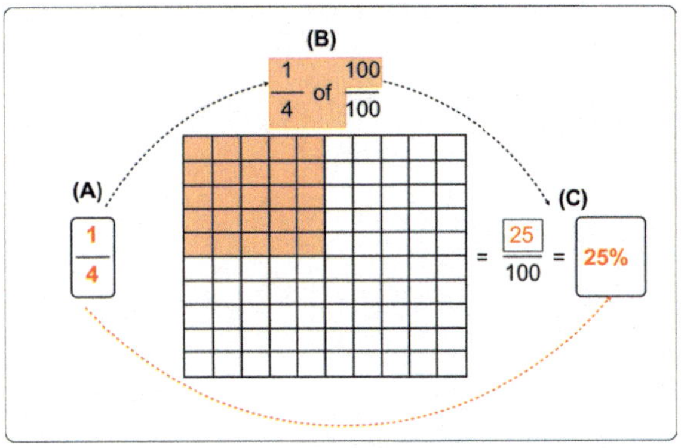

Just as ¼ is the same as 25%, similarly ½ is the same as 2-quarters which amounts to 50%:

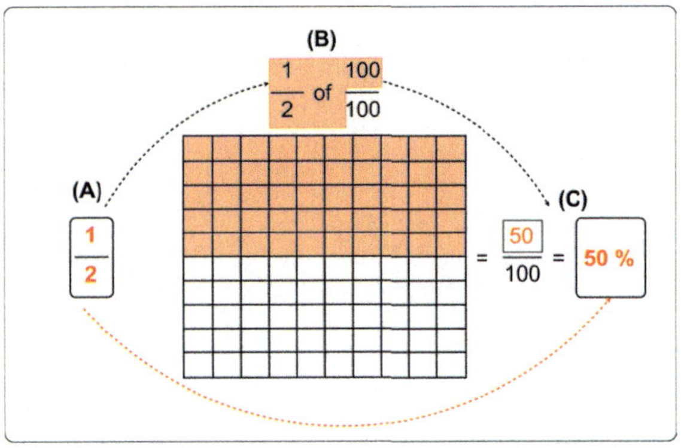

... and ¾ (3-quarters) is the same as 75%:

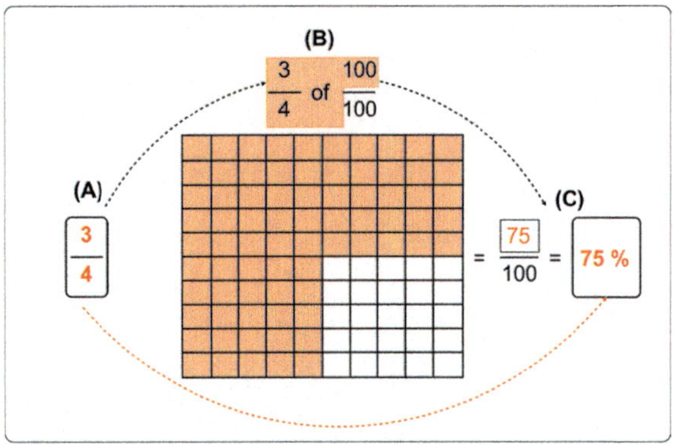

In Stage 4, "*Mathematical Operations*", we will zoom in for a closer, wide-angled look at how mathematical operations involving percentages have informed the world we live in. Percentage reduces all fractions into a single standard size. We will see how everything and anything that is measurable, can be mathematically broken into a hundred equal parts, and for very good reasons, too.

CONCLUSION

WHY MATHEMATICS FEELS SO DIFFICULT !

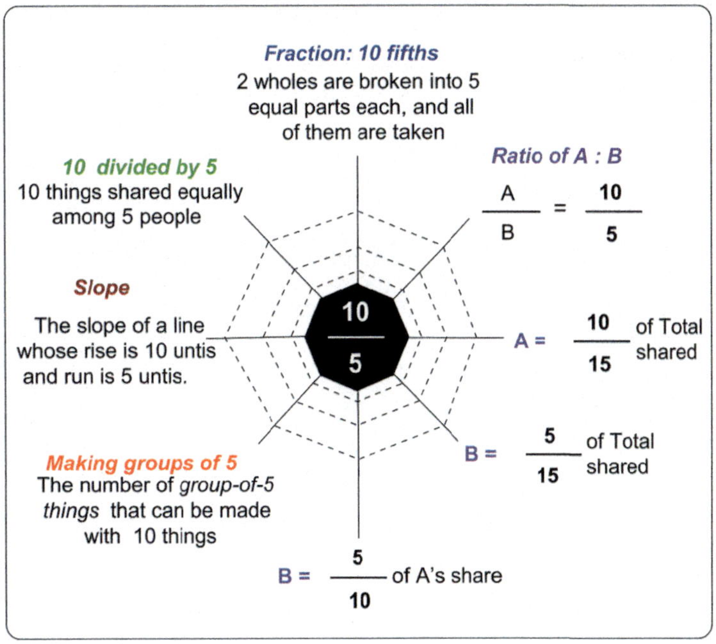

Myths like "Math is difficult" or it "requires a special aptitude" etc are associated with historical inconsistencies in math teaching. The fraction template shown in black at the centre, lies at the heart of a web of mathematical connections. Eight distinct conceptual universes are embodied in this template. Each universe has its own set of rules, quite different from the others. We can add percentage to it, as the ninth conceptual universe for further exploration.

Many well-intentioned practitioners mistakenly extrapolate multiple concepts simultaneously into their teaching. The encode and decode them freely, as they appear in their discourse. This entails a lot of explanations and clarifications that cause the learner's initial clarity and understanding to get hopelessly fuzzy. Learners move rapidly from one world to another in a daze. It's like first entering a cave, then sliding down a desert dune and splash into the sea, then suddenly get lifted up to the clouds, before plunging into a snowy mountain top. The confusion that follows is inescapable.

The Deep Knowledge System catches passing glimpses of the sea, interspersed with snapshots of the desert, the dark waters, a passing cloud, and flashes of snowy mountain tops. Understandably, the rules for negotiating such different terrains keep changing. Decoding fractions differently from how it was encoded is a sure-fire recipe for producing instructional inconsistencies. Our Deep Knowledge System is unable to respond to them. Cognitive processes, when declogged, offer many rewards. Far less time and labour is expended on trying to understand math.

Mastery requires the encoding and decoding of conceptual understanding across the tri-sensory modalities of sight, sound and speech. This can only be done when all three are provoked to a degree where responses appear in a snap, on demand, through any mode:

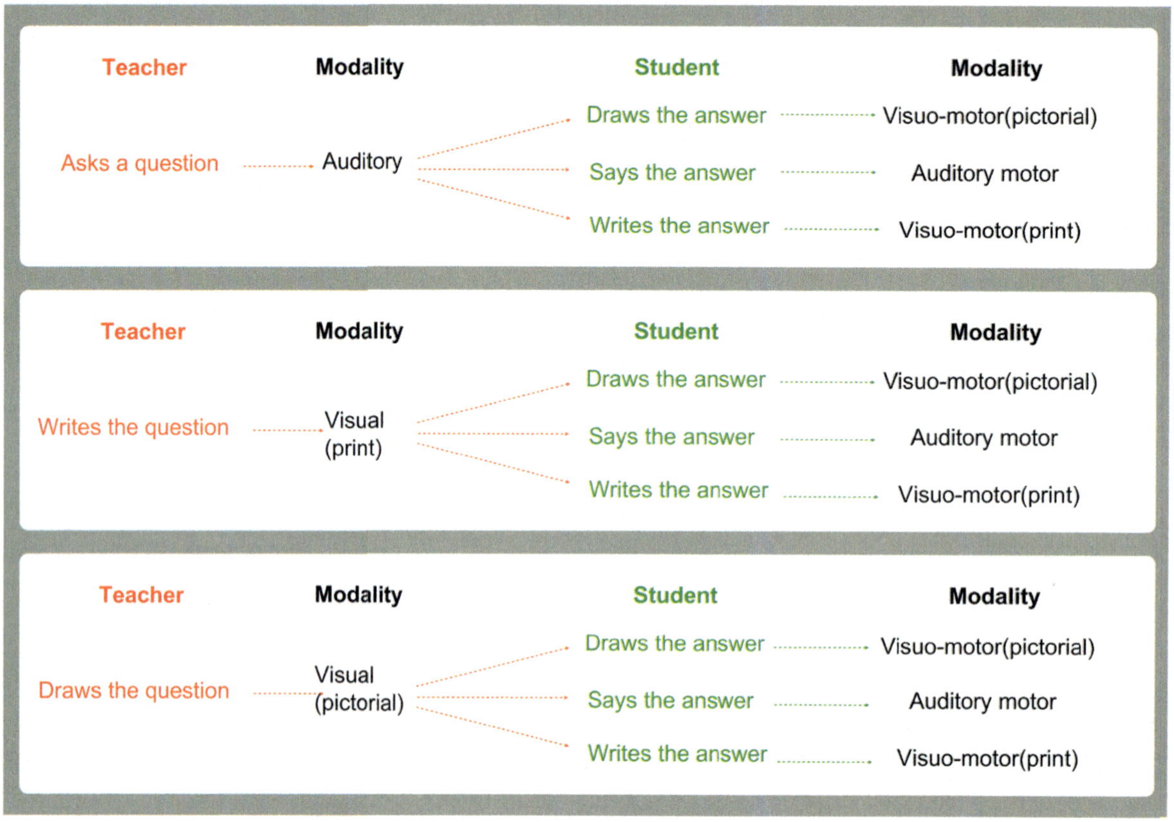

We have seen how the Fraction template (TAKE over BREAK) is sounded and read differently in varying contexts as "fifths", sometimes "slope", or "ratio", then as "divide" or "equal grouping" and also as "percent"! Teachers should be cautious when decoding symbols that are used to "mathematise" different math concepts. Teaching how to encode them will reduce the number of mathematical errors quite substantially.

If a math concept that has been encoded in a certain way is mistakenly decoded by learners in another way, it offers room for very precise investigation by the teacher, parent, trainer or diagnostician. It is like knowing four different people named "Sam". When reading about a certain "Sam" we are able identify quite correctly, the personality, behaviour and appearance of the intended Sam. We can do this only if we know all four Sam's equally well. When learners partake in the encoding of mathematical concepts like first-time learners, all the way up to mastery levels, their intimate knowledge of each process makes it easy for them to decode different mathematical concepts correctly.

APPENDIX A

The Power of Visualization

A picture is worth a thousand words... *and* numbers, when we try to think mathematically. One has to use a lot of words and numbers to explain the difference between division as *equal sharing* and division as *equal grouping*. It is because mathematics engages both numerical and verbal reasoning. The two run alongside, entwine, criss-cross, meet or part ways. All these behaviours are deliberate and precise, and a slight change in accent can cause a change in meaning. When explaining the difference between "factors" and "factoring" a teacher has to consider the mathematical context which itself may require clarification. All that I have said so far can be demonstrated via one or two carefully crafted, evocative visuals.

Mathematical concepts provoke visualisation and a lot of them consist of dynamic imagery, of ideas caught in motion, connections that remain stable and understandable while moving from one state to another. They collapse when the motion ceases, or slows down below a certain threshold of speed. Of course, the visualisation has to make sense even when not mathematical. For instance, you can show a static shot of a figure jumping off a 60 feet high diving board into an olympic pool. The next figure is shown falling vertically, head down, arms outstretched. The last one shows the splash that follows, with just the feet showing. If this was shown visually, you wouldn't have to read so many words to visualise it. You would get it at a glance, within seconds, freeing up time to think about it and even feel it.

If the last shot showed the diver in a horizontal position just before hitting the water, it will leave you wondering: "*That makes no sense*". It's because you are reasoning visually.

Visual reasoning holds the key to unraveling math concepts. In long, broad strokes, the images displace pages of printed words while inviting both verbal and numerical reasoning. When combined with principles of Universal Design in Learning (UDL), the learning of mathematics can turn into a pleasant immersive experience.

For instance, imagine a tube with an open top in frame 1. The transparent one is shown on the left, and the opaque one on the right. Above it is a clutter of jellybeans. The jellybeans are stored in the tubes. The tubes are labeled "T" for Tube:

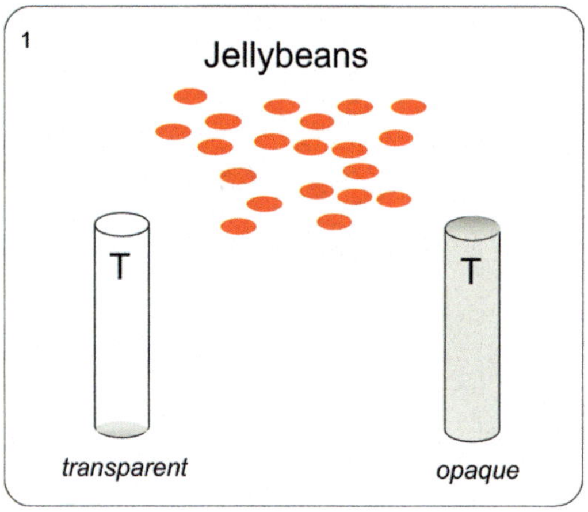

Myra and Kian are playing an interesting game. Myra has 3 empty tubes and Kian has 2:

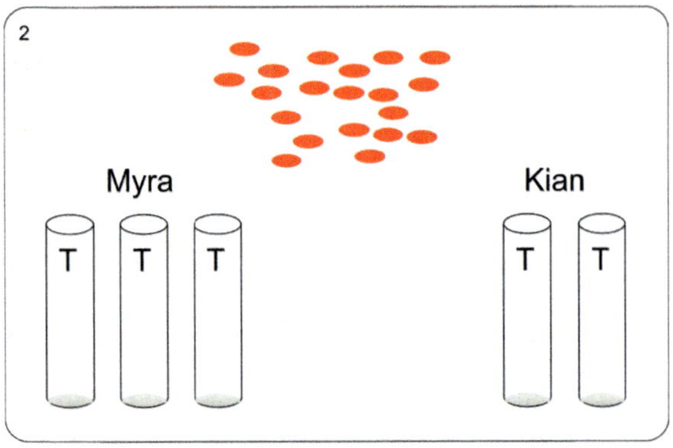

Then Myra takes 3 jellybeans, and Kian takes 5:

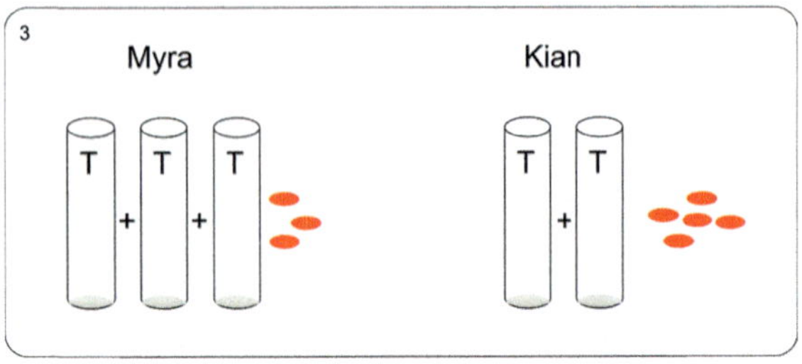

Goal of the game: Each has to put the same number of jelly beans inside each tube so that the total number of jellybeans (inside and outside the tubes) are the same for Myra and Kian. How many jellybeans should go in each tube?

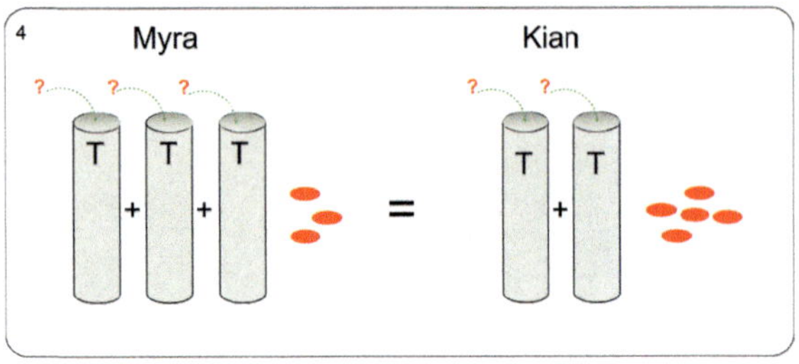

They began first by putting 1 jellybean in each tube:

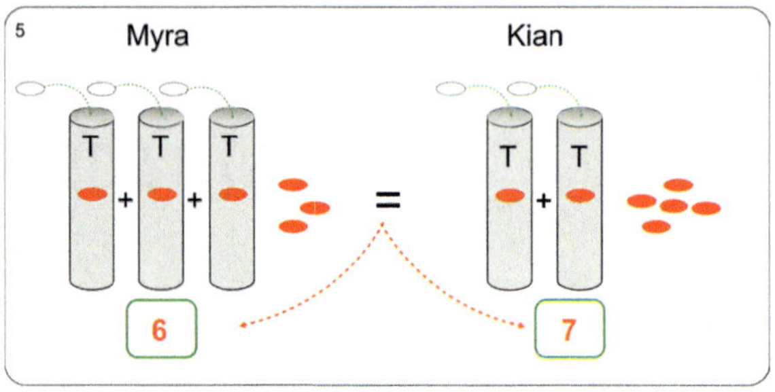

It didn't work, because Myra got 6 and Kian got 7 jellybeans. They were not equal. So they put another jellybean into each tube:

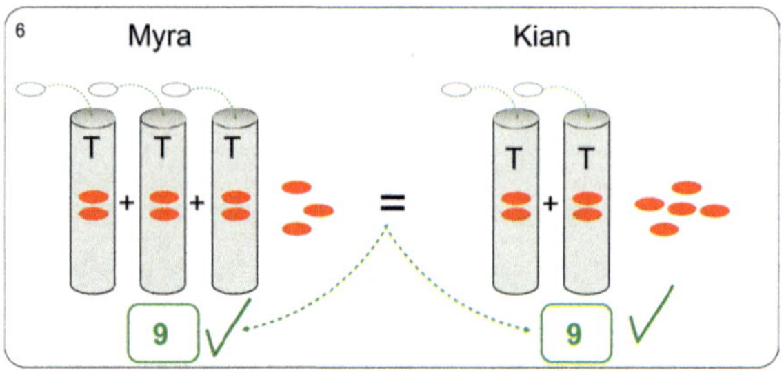

It worked with 2 beans in each tube. Each of them got 9 beans. Is there a smarter, quicker and surer way than trial-and-error, to find out how many beans should go in each tube so each ends up with an equal number of jellybeans?

Here is how: All you need to know is that if you remove the same amounts from Myra and Kian, each will continue to have equal amounts.

Rule for Step 1: Remove the same number of tubes from Myra's and Kian's side. Make sure it is the most you can remove:

STEP 1

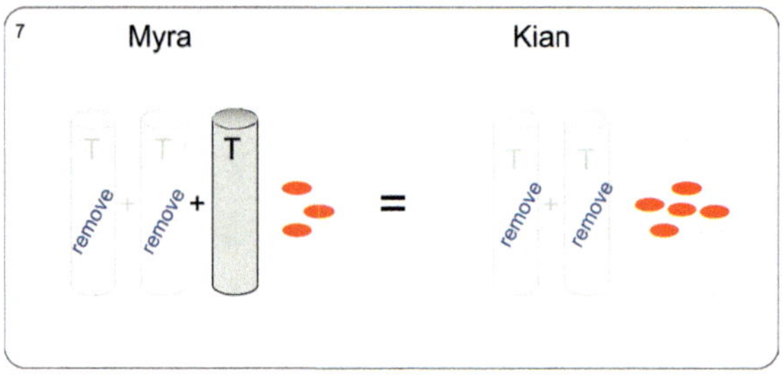

After removing 2 tubes from each side, Myra is left with 1 tube and 3 jellybeans. Kian is left with just 5 jelly beans.

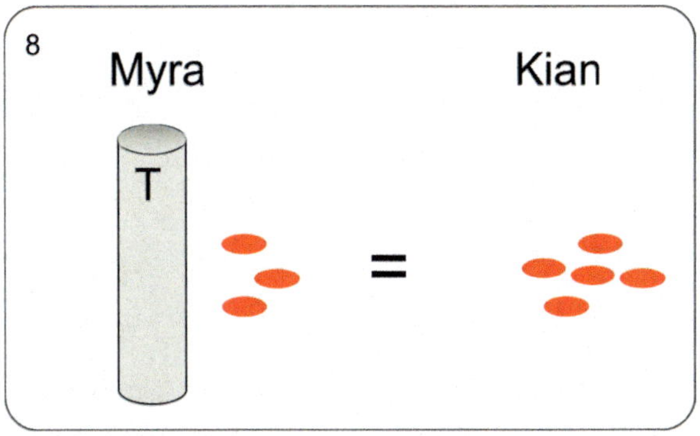

Rule for Step 2: Remove the *same number* of jelly beans from each side. Make sure it is the most you can remove so that 1 person is left with just jelly beans:

STEP 2

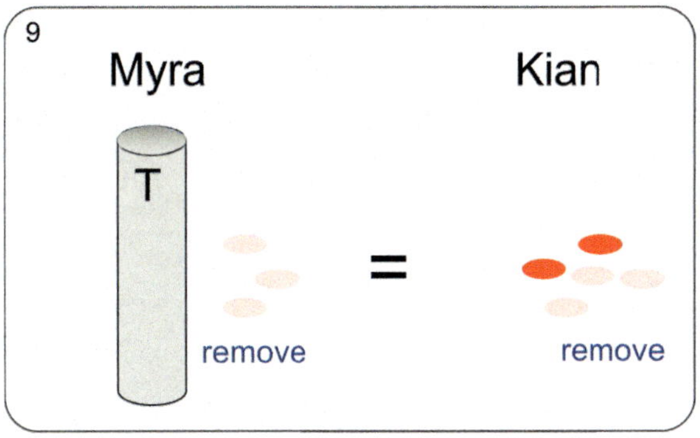

After removing 3 jellybeans from each side, Myra and Kian are left with the same number of jellybeans, 2 each:

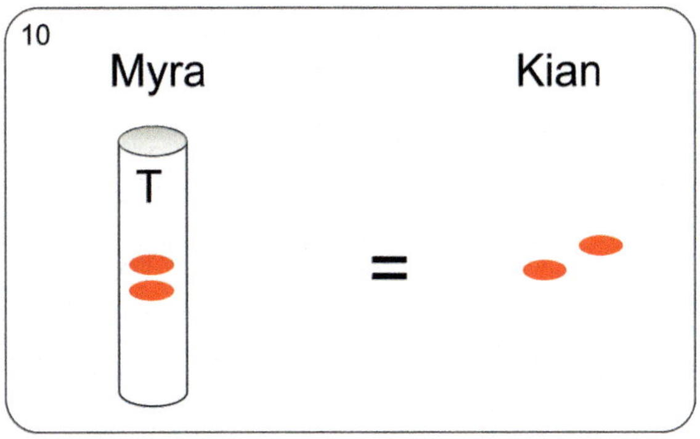

The solution is staring at us. Each tube must have 2 jellybeans. Let us check to make sure:

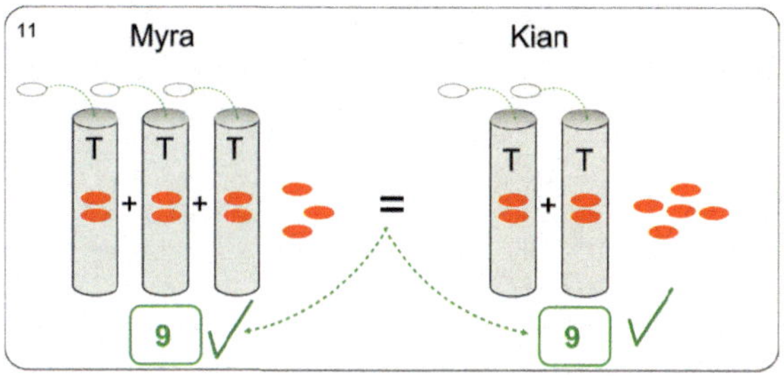

Yes, it is correct. Each gets 9 jelly beans. The earlier trial-and-error approach gave the same solution.

Let us look at it mathematically. The problem being posed is shown in the left frame. The right frame shows Step 1 when two tubes (or 2T's) are removed from each side:

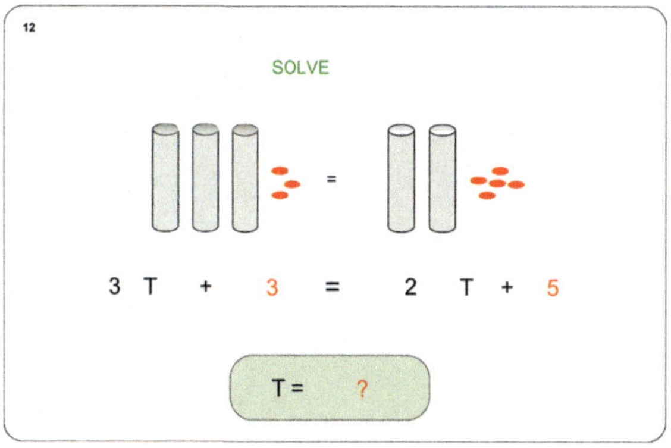

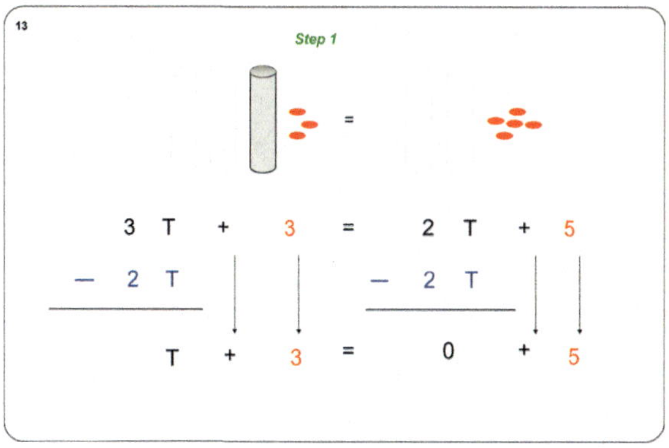

In Step 2, three beans (or 3) are removed from each side:

The answer is T = 2.

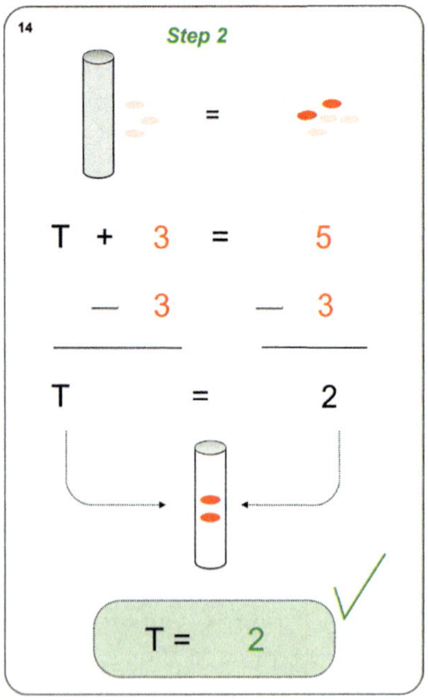

In Algebra we show it very formally in this way. Here, *x* represents a tube, or T.

$$3x + 3 = 2x + 5$$

Step 1 → $3x + 3 - 2x = 2x + 5 - 2x$

$$3x - 2x + 3 = 2x - 2x + 5$$

$$x + 3 = 5$$

Step 2 → $x + 3 - 3 = 5 - 3$

$$x = 2$$

Now try this one. Find out how many jellybeans should go inside each tube:

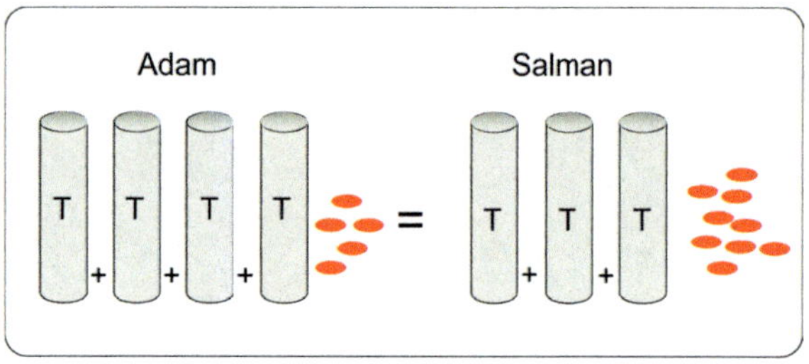

Try the trial-n-error method first, then the smarter one, using the algebraic approach of removing the same amount from each side, first the T's then the beans. Of course, you can get the answer within minutes just by studying the graphic and scribbling numbers on paper. You will be reasoning visually, verbally, numerically and even abstractly.

But mathematics is not just about getting the right answers. It is about declaring one's intention and planning, about demonstrating one's skill at making executive decisions that can be defended by logic and reasoning and recording them as mathematical statements (as in the frame on the left). At the end of the day, the easiest way to dispel anxiety is to know what you are doing, why you are doing it, and how *you* chose to do it. It fosters respect for other innovative ways of doing it.

Acknowledgments

The Six Stages are being published as six separate books.

My special thanks to Anjana Raza, my wife whose editorial inputs were invaluable. This work wouldn't be possible without her continued support throughout my most challenging phases in completing the Six Stages.

I also thank Dr. Thomas Oberlechner, Dr. Gerlinde Berghofer, Dr. Paul Goldenberg (EDC, U.S.A), Dr. Herbert Ginsberg (Professor, Columbia University), Julie Diamond (U.S.A), Zenna Hopkins (former Chairperson, OFSTED, UK), and Mary Tang (Singapore), for all their support and faith in my struggle to bring it to fruition.

Finally, my immense gratitude to all my students, parents and teachers in different parts of the world who inspired this work. All the foundational elements in my work have been drawn from my readings of the following giants in the field of education, psychology and neuro-cognition:

1. Piaget and Vygotsky
2. Alan Bishop and Norma Presmeg
3. W.W. Sawyer
4. Stephen M Brown and Marion Walter
5. Dr. Jeanne Chall
6. Chris Argyris
7. Donald Schoen
8. Anna Sfard
9. Tobias Danzig
10. Stanislas Dehaene
11. David A. Souza
12. David Rose
13. Barbel Inhelder
14. Paul Goldenberg
15. Elizabeth Spelke

Additional (most recent) influences:
- Abu Ja'far Muhammad ibn Musa al-Al-Khwarazmi's: Book – *Algebra*
- Abel Fath Omar Bin-Al-Khayyam: Book – *On Algebra and Equations*
- Imam al-Haramayn al-Juwayni: Book – *A Guide to Conclusive Proof for the Principles of Belief*

SHAD MOARIF, Ed.M
Founder-Developer, Karismath
Woking, Surrey, United Kingdom
September 26, 2022

Printed in Great Britain
by Amazon

15744791R00061